SECRETS
OF THE
EARTH

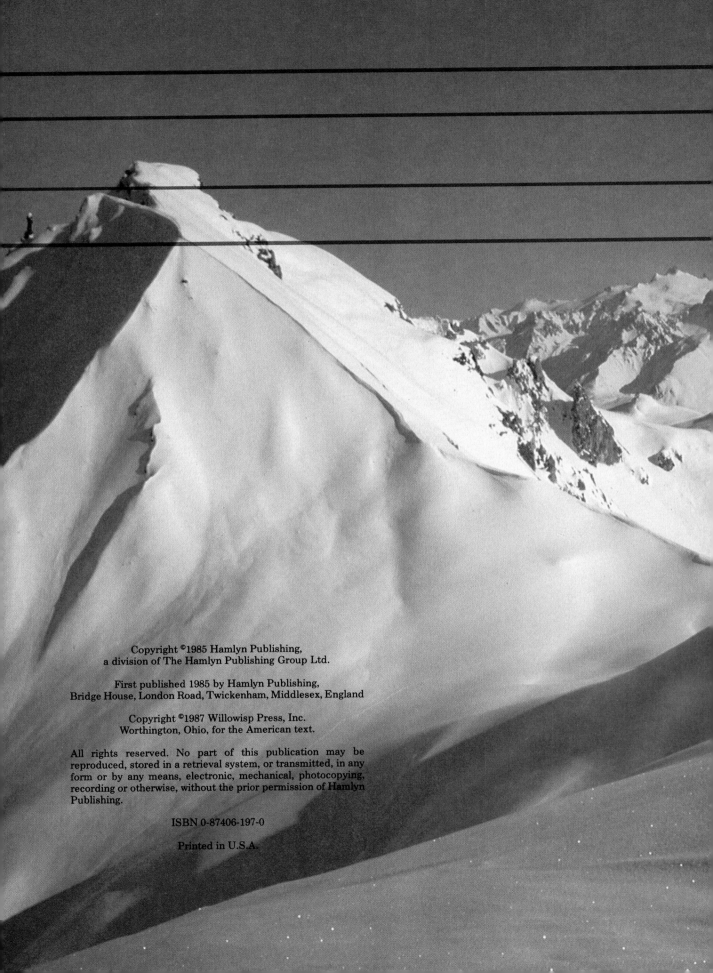

ISBN 0-87406-197-0

Printed in U.S.A.

SECRETS
OF THE
EARTH

DOUGAL DIXON

Willowisp
Press

CONTENTS

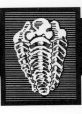

PLATE TECTONICS

THE EARTH'S ITCHY SKIN

Christopher Columbus crossed the Atlantic in 1492. He became the first recorded European to set foot in America. His perilous voyage of discovery took him 70 days. If he did the same voyage today it would take him a little longer. Today, North America and Europe are farther apart. The Atlantic Ocean is now about 33 feet (10 meters) wider than it was in Columbus' time!

The other continents are also moving on the surface of the earth. The oceans are continually widening and narrowing. Most of them are doing so faster than the Atlantic did between 1492 and today.

But how can this be? We cannot feel the continents moving. They seem to be solid immovable masses of rock. In fact, the mechanism for the movement lies at the bottom of the sea. This is why scientists knew nothing about it until the 1960's.

THE PANELED EARTH

Imagine a pan of boiling jam. Hot liquid rises in the center, moves around, and sinks again. Scum or froth moves around on the surface but does not sink. This is what is happening to the continents. The ocean floor is constantly being renewed. Hot material from the interior of the earth wells up along lines of weakness in the seabed. It then solidifies to form a new ocean floor. This new ocean floor then moves away and is swallowed up and destroyed in other regions. The result is that the earth's crust is composed of a number of separate plates, like the panels of a soccer ball. Each panel is continually being generated along one seam and being destroyed along another. The continents are made of a lighter material than the ocean floor. They sit embedded in the ocean plates and are carried along wherever the currents move the plates.

Earth scientists call this process "plate tectonics." The upwelling sites lie along submarine ocean ridges. The old material is destroyed in the deep trenches found at the edges of many of the oceans. At the trenches, one plate slides over another and the lower one is destroyed beneath.

The continents cannot sink at these sites. So, when a moving continent reaches a trench, it sits there while the next ocean plate disappears

We can divide the earth's surface into a number of plates, each one moving in relation to the others.

Map showing plate movement and boundaries

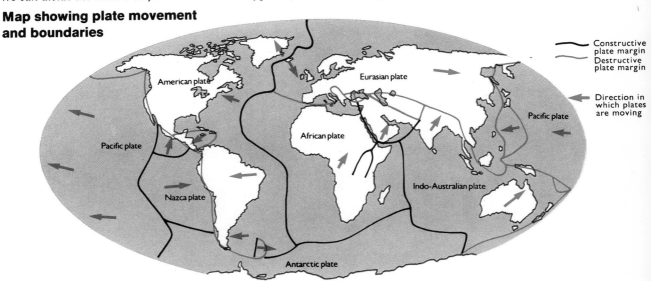

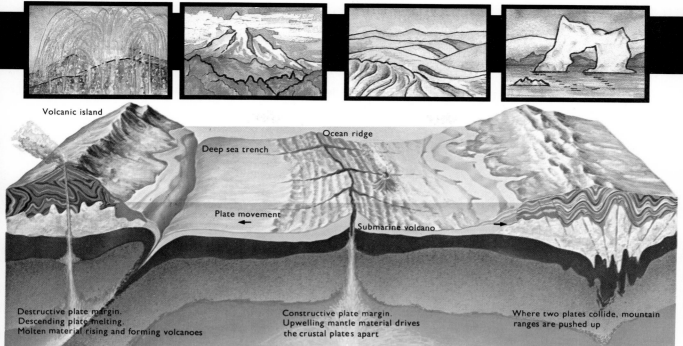

Volcanic island

Ocean ridge

Deep sea trench

Plate movement

←

Submarine volcano

→

Destructive plate margin.
Descending plate melting.
Molten material rising and forming volcanoes

Constructive plate margin.
Upwelling mantle material drives
the crustal plates apart

Where two plates collide, mountain
ranges are pushed up

The movement of tectonic plates

Hot material rising from below the crust at oceanic ridges forms the plates. These plates then move apart. When plates collide they form ocean trenches or mountains.

beneath. This is what is happening along the western coast of South America. The volcanoes and the mountains of the Andes are a direct result of this activity.

There are also volcanoes at the ocean ridges where new crust material is being formed. However, these all lie at great depths, so we do not often see them.

Where two ocean plates collide, volcanoes form a curved chain of islands. The Mariana Islands of the western Pacific formed this way.

Occasionally two continents will collide, forming a huge mountain chain between them. The Himalayas formed like this when India collided with the rest of Asia less than 50 million years ago.

How the theory of plate tectonics developed

If we look at the continents of Africa and South America, we would almost think that we were looking at two pieces of a jigsaw puzzle. It seems obvious that the "nose" of South America could fit snugly into the bays of the western coast of Africa. Many people have pointed this out throughout history, but most scientists disregarded this idea of "continental drift." Nobody knew of a force powerful enough to rip continents apart and move them across the globe.

Then, in the 1960's, oceanographers discovered that the rocks of the ocean bed were quite young in the area of the oceanic ridges. The rocks became older farther away. This proved that the ocean floors were constantly being generated. At last, there was a method by which the continents could be moved. This new idea of "seafloor spreading" was combined with the older idea of "continental drift" to form the modern concept of "plate tectonics."

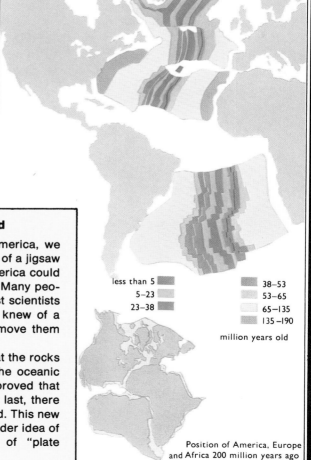

less than 5

5–23

23–38

38–53

53–65

65–135

135–190

million years old

Position of America, Europe and Africa 200 million years ago

CUTTING UP THE BIG BALL

The earth has an average diameter of 7,920 miles (12,742 kilometers). The deepest that we have ever been able to reach below the surface by drilling is 7.5 miles (12 kilometers). That is less than one five-hundredth of the distance to the center. What, then, do we know about the interior of the earth?

Scientists have discovered that it is divided into layers. At the center are the inner and the outer cores. They are surrounded by the mantle. This comprises the greatest part of the earth's bulk. The core and mantle are separated by the Gutenberg discontinuity. Then, as a thin rind relatively no thicker than the skin of an apple, we have the crust. The crust is the only part that we can see and sample directly. It is separated from the mantle by the Mohorovičič discontinuity, or Moho.

The crust of the continents consists mainly of *si*licon and *al*uminum, so it is called sial. The crust of the ocean floor is slightly denser than that of the continents. The oceanic crust is called sima after its main constituents, *si*licon and *ma*gnesium. The mantle is denser, but it is still made of stony material with a great deal of the element silicon in it. The core, however, is quite different. It is probably made of iron. The outer core is liquid, while the inner core is probably solid.

The outer core is the only liquid part of the earth's structure (with the exception of the oceans). However, there is a zone of soft, moveable material near the top of the mantle. This squashy layer enables the plates of the earth's surface to move. The plates themselves consist of oceanic and continental crust and the upper layer of the mantle. This thin, rigid layer is called the lithosphere. The soft layer beneath that lubricates the plates is called the asthenosphere.

Lithosphere (solid) Up to 60 miles (100 km) thick
Asthenosphere (squashy) 60 miles (100 km) thick

Crust

Mantle (mostly solid)

Asthenosph
rises to surfa
beneath ocean
ridge

Cross section through the earth

Cross section through the lithosphere

1,800 miles
(2,885 km)

Outer core (liquid)

The earth's solid core is 755 miles (1,215 kilometers) in radius. The liquid outer core is 1,410 miles (2,270 kilometers) thick. The stony mantle has a thickness of 1,647 miles (2,850 kilometers). The oceanic crust is between 3-6 miles (5-10 kilometers) thick, while the continental crust is between 15-56 miles (25-90 kilometers) thick.

Inner core (solid)

3,200 miles
(5,155 km)

Center 3,950 miles
(6,370 km)

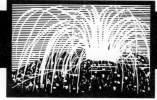

Meteorites are made of the same materials that built the earth. They can tell us what lies beneath the crust.

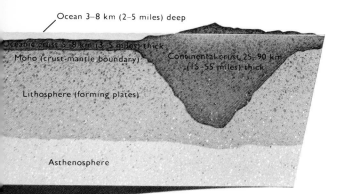

Ocean 3–8 km (2–5 miles) deep

Oceanic crust 5–8 km (3–5 miles) thick

Moho (crust-mantle boundary)

Continental crust 25–90 km (15–55 miles) thick

Lithosphere (forming plates)

Asthenosphere

How do we know all this if we can see only about 7.5 miles (12 kilometers) into the earth? Earthquakes provide the answer. The shock of an earthquake can send vibrations through the earth. These vibrations are called seismic waves. They can be measured on sensitive instruments all over the world. The different kinds of seismic waves travel at different speeds and along different paths through different materials. The pattern of waves emerging at the other side of the earth from an earthquake can tell us what kind of materials the waves passed through.

Meteorites can also give clues as to what the earth is like inside because they are small pieces left over from the formation of the solar system. Everything in the solar system was made from the same cloud of gas and dust that existed before the sun was born. This includes the earth and the other planets, the moons, the asteroids, and the meteorites. When the earth solidified, the heaviest parts of the raw material probably sank to the core, while the lightest parts remained on the outside. There are two types of meteorites: stony and iron. Scientists believe that stony meteorites are made from the light minerals that formed the mantle and the crust, while iron meteorites are made from the same material that sank to form the core.

Earthquakes—insights into the earth's interior

An earthquake is a sudden disturbance in the crust of the earth. It sets off a series of vibrations like the ripples in a pond after a stone has been thrown in. Several kinds of earthquake waves are produced. The most important are the P waves (produced by pressure) and the S waves (giving a shaking action). These are deflected as they pass through layers of different density in the earth. Both produce particular patterns as they reappear at the surface. Also, the S waves cannot travel through liquid. They are stopped by a liquid layer. Therefore the pattern of earthquake waves recorded during an earthquake can show us where the layers of different densities lie and whether or not these layers are solid.

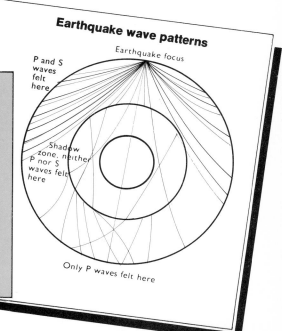

Earthquake wave patterns

Earthquake focus

P and S waves felt here

Shadow zone, neither P nor S waves felt here

Only P waves felt here

CONTINENTS

THE STONY RAFTS

If you travel around the countryside you will see all sorts of different landscapes. You may see tall mountains in one place. A few miles away, you may see flat plains with rivers winding gracefully across them. Then, still close by, you may see hills covered in forests. You would almost think that the surface of the earth is a haphazard array of different landscapes.

This first impression would be wrong. If you could stand back far enough, you would be able to see the underlying pattern. The astronauts on board the *Space Shuttle* and the cosmonauts on board the *Soyuz* space capsules are lucky enough to be able to do this. The rest of us, including earth-bound scientists, can only look at pictures and measurements taken by space probes and satellites.

These show us that the continents are mostly flat in the middle and have mountains around the edges. North America is a good example. In the center are the prairies. The prairies are vast, flat, wheat-growing areas that stretch from the Midwest of the United States northward into the flat wildernesses of northern Canada. To the east there is the mountain chain of the Appalachians. To the west are the mountain chains of the Rockies and the Coast Ranges.

Geologists can study the rocks of each of these areas and find out how old they are. The flat areas in the center are made up of hard, old rocks that are thousands of millions of years old. The mountains around the outside are younger. The closer they are to the edge, the younger they are. It is almost as if the continents started off as the hard lump in the middle and have been growing ever since, with mountain ranges added around the outside. That is exactly what has been happening.

HOW CONTINENTS GROW

As the continents move around on the surface of the earth, they often come to rest where one plate is sliding beneath another. New mountains are squeezed up from the sediments of the sea and are pierced by volcanoes. The mountains increase the area of the continent.

However, the picture is not quite as simple as this. If you look at a map of Africa, you will see a long valley stretching up the eastern side of the continent, from Mozambique to the Red Sea. This is the Great Rift Valley. Africa is, literally, being torn apart along this valley. A new constructive plate margin is developing below the continent here. Sometime in the future Africa will split in two. The smaller eastern section will drift into the Indian Ocean. This has happened before. The reason that the eastern coast of South America and the western coast of Africa are the same shape is that they were once a single continent. They broke apart 150 million years ago when a new constructive plate margin began to form the Atlantic Ocean.

Sometimes continents collide. The Himalayas are the greatest mountains on the earth. They were thrown up when the moving continent of India crashed into the massive continent of Asia 50 million years ago. Before this, Europe

Cross section through a theoretical continent

| deep sea trench destructive plate margin | New fold mountains and volcanoes near deep sea trench (e.g. Andes) | Older fold mountains further inland (e.g. Rockies) | Ancient metamorphic rock eroded flat (craton) and covered with undisturbed sedimentary rock (e.g. American prairies) | Old fold mountains formed where two continents fused together (e.g. Urals) | Craton with no sedimentary cover (e.g. Canadian Shield) | Rift valley, where new constructive plate margin is pulling the continent apart (e.g. East African Rift Valley) | Continental shelf showing rift structures, relics of the rift valley that formed as this continent separated from another (e.g. east coast of North America) |

anic crust

ement

collided with Asia about 300 million years ago. The Urals were crushed up between the two continents. The Urals are now not as high as the Himalayas because they have had much more time to be eroded.

Continents (above) are built of hard, old rocks worn flat into plains (below) and new rocks still crumpled into mountains (right). The continents may be pulled apart in rift valleys. The rift structures may still exist at the edges, showing where they once broke away from a larger mass. The newest mountains are found at one edge, where converging plates crush up the continental margin.

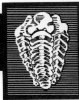

FOLDS AND FAULTS

THE ITCHES SCRATCHED

A piece of rock may seem to be a hard, solid object. It seems unbelievable that the rocks of the earth's surface could bend and twist like dough.

FOLDS, BENT ROCKS

Rocks do bend and twist under the great forces that move the continents. You can see the results. The rocks of mountains and road cuts show layers of originally horizontal rocks that have been crumpled, twisted, and wrenched into all sorts of fantastic shapes. This is the result of compressional stress. That means the rocks have been pushed in from each side. If you have several layers of paper or cloth on a table, and you push the edges toward each other, the layers wrinkle and then crumple up in the middle, giving the same sorts of structures. Geologists call these structures folds. When geological folds sag in the middle, they are called synclines. When they arch up, they are called anticlines. You do not usually get one without the other. They are normally both found in a region where the rocks are folded repeatedly.

FAULTS, CRACKED ROCKS

Sometimes the rocks do not fold. They break instead. When this happens, the result is known as a fault. Faults can be just a yard or two long. They can stretch for many hundreds of miles, like the San Andreas fault in California.

It is easy to recognize a fault in the rock. It looks like a crack along which two masses of rock have moved. A fault can be caused by compressional forces, like those that produce folds. More often, they are caused by tensional stresses, where the rocks have pulled apart.

As with folds, there are usually many faults in a particular area. Sometimes the rock between two faults has slipped down. This gives a structure called a graben. If the rock between two faults has moved up, it results in a structure called a horst. These structures may have an effect on the landscape above. A cliff that forms along a fault is called a fault scarp. A depression produced by a graben is called a rift valley, like the one in eastern Africa. When a horst produces a hill, the hill is called a block mountain.

Different technical terms describe the different ways and directions in which folds and faults occur. The different types can be easily recognized.

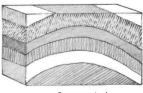

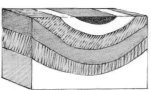
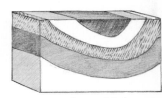

Symmetrical   Asymmetrical   **Folds**   Symmetrical   Asymmetrical
Anticline   Syncline

Faults

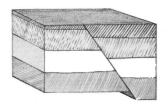
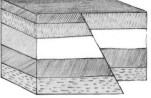
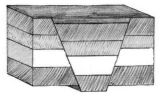
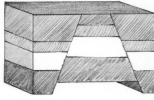

Normal fault produced by tension   Reverse fault produced by compression   Graben   Horst

These structures do not usually show at the surface. Erosion keeps the surface landscape flat

12

These folded limestones in the Swiss Jura show both a syncline and an anticline. The fault (left) in Kenya is a normal fault. The block on the right obviously moved downward.

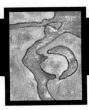 

MOUNTAINS

THE WRINKLES IN THE SKIN

The Himalayas are the tallest mountains on the earth. Mount Everest, the greatest of these, remained remote and unclimbed until 1953. The Andes, along the western edge of South America, are the longest chain of mountains in the world. They extend 5,500 miles (8,900 kilometers) from well north of the equator to the Antarctic Circle.

All the world's religions have stories about mountains. Mountains are traditionally regarded as the dwelling-places of gods or giants. Even today, in modern stories, mountains play the part of mysterious and impenetrable barriers. Tarzan was hidden from the outside world by a jungle mountain range. In a story by Sir Arthur Conan Doyle, the Lost World with its surviving dinosaurs was perched on top of a remote mountain.

Yet the mountains of the world are really quite insignificant when we look at the world as a whole. The earth is 7,920 miles (12,742 kilometers) in diameter. The tallest mountain is only 29,028 feet (8.85 kilometers) high. The great mountain chains of the world hardly blemish the perfect sphere of the earth. Even the great Mount Everest is not as high as the Pacific Ocean is deep. The Pacific is 35,960 feet (11.03 kilometers) deep.

Nevertheless, to us, the mountains are vast and imposing. They can be formed in three different ways.

THREE TYPES OF MOUNTAINS

The highest and most extensive ranges of mountains today are the fold mountains. These are formed at the edges of continents, where the stony rafts push against the moving plates of the oceans or crash into one another. They are formed from sandstones, mudstones, and limestones. These are the rocks that have gathered on the sea bottom near the continental margins. The rocks are highly distorted and folded. The surfaces of fold mountains are not the smooth and rounded surfaces seen in diagrams. They are rough and jagged, forming sharp ridges and broken peaks, and deep valleys and gorges. This is because winds, rains, frosts, and rivers attack the mountains to wear them down again. All mountains are in a state of decay.

The second type of mountain is the block mountain. This is formed when a mass of rock has been forced upward between two faults or when the surrounding land has subsided, leaving a block in the middle at the original height. Like the fold mountains, block mountains do not look like the simple diagrams that are used to show their formation. They too are attacked by the weather and worn back. Block mountains are less extensive than fold mountains and are often found in the centers of continents. The mountains along the Great Rift Valley in eastern Africa are block mountains. They were thrust up by the underlying plate tectonic forces that are splitting the continent apart.

The third type of mountain is the volcanic mountain. During an eruption, ash and lava thrown out of the volcano increase its height. Although these mountains tend to be spectacular, they are not very important as far as

Fold Mountains

Severe deformation
near crustal impact

Gentle deformation further away

Theoretical

Pressure

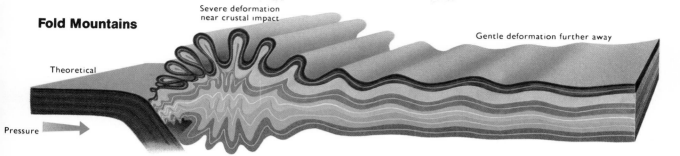

Eroded jagged peaks   e.g. Alps

Rolling hills   e.g. English downs

Actual

Pressure

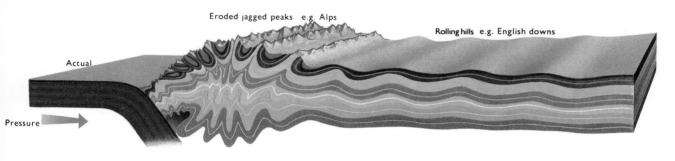

Block Mountains

Theoretical

Actual

Surface features are worn away by erosion and partly obscured
by a covering of eroded material

the relief of the globe is concerned. They are usually found in areas of other types of mountain building. Volcanoes occur where the earth movements are bringing hot material to the surface through weaknesses produced by folding and through the faults of the block mountains.

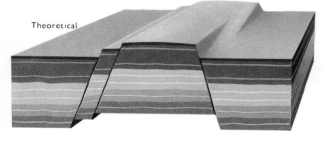

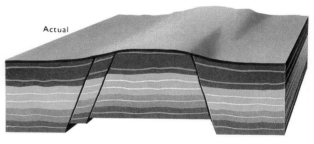

Of the three types of mountains, only the fold mountains (top) are of any real significance in the geography of the earth. The fold mountains form the great mountain chains of the world. The block mountains (above) are usually associated with rift valleys. They are sometimes found in the centers of the continents where the rocks are too old and compact to fold. Volcanic mountains, such as those in the Philippines (left), form along plate margins in response to movements between the plates.

EARTHQUAKES

WHEN THE SKIN SHIVERS

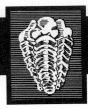

"6,000 DEAD IN MEXICO CITY," announce the headlines. "EARTHQUAKE SHAKES CENTRAL CHINA—280,000 KILLED."

The earth has been moving throughout history. Many hundreds died when the city of San Francisco was destroyed by an earthquake in 1906. When the plates move on the crust of the earth, they throw up mountain ranges and split continents apart. It is not surprising that all this activity can have a devastating effect on the people who live nearby.

Usually, the plates do not move in one continuous glide. Faults do not appear and creep gradually to their present positions in a smooth imperceptible slide through millions of years. Instead, earth movements tend to be sudden events. One plate pushing against another for several years builds up stresses and pressures.

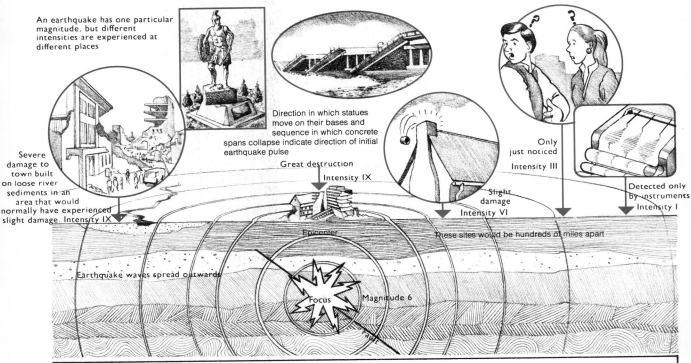

An earthquake has one particular magnitude, but different intensities are experienced at different places

Direction in which statues move on their bases and sequence in which concrete spans collapse indicate direction of initial earthquake pulse

Great destruction
Intensity IX

Only just noticed
Intensity III

Severe damage to town built on loose river sediments in an area that would normally have experienced slight damage. Intensity IX

Slight damage
Intensity VI

Detected only by instruments
Intensity I

Epicenter

These sites would be hundreds of miles apart

Earthquake waves spread outwards

Focus

Magnitude 6

Fault

How do we measure earthquakes?

One method is to observe the actual effect an earthquake has. This tells us the degree of the earthquake's *intensity*. This varies from place to place. An earthquake is most intense at its epicenter. We can measure the intensity on a 12-point scale called the Mercalli scale.

I. Felt only by instruments.

II. You feel it if you are upstairs. Lightbulbs swing.

III. You feel the earthquake indoors.

IV. You feel it outdoors. If you are inside it feels like a truck hitting the building, making windows rattle.

V. It wakes you up if you are asleep and cracks the plaster.

VI. Windows and dishes break and plaster falls.

VII. It is difficult to stand, and loose bricks fall.

VIII. Chimneys fall down, and you can't steer a car.

IX. The ground cracks, and buildings collapse.

X. All houses are smashed, and landslides start.

XI. Railway lines bend, and bridges and underground pipes are destroyed.

XII. You would be lucky to survive this one. Objects are thrown into the air and everything is destroyed.

All this depends on where you are. Geologists prefer to use a scale of *magnitude,* which is a measure of the total energy released by the earthquake. An earthquake may have a whole range of intensities, but only one magnitude. The Richter scale is used to measure this. Each spacing on the scale represents 30 times as much energy as the one before. Hence an earthquake measuring 5 on the Richter scale is 30 times as great as one measuring 4. It is 900 times as great as one measuring 3. Few earthquakes have ever been recorded that were greater than 8 on the scale.

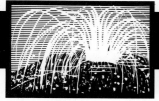

Eventually the force becomes so great that the rock snaps. The plates jump an inch or so to their new positions. They may remain there for another few years, or even centuries, until the stress builds up again.

When the breaking point comes, it sends vibrations through the crust of the earth. The vibrations spread away from the point of the break like ripples on a pond after a splash. These vibrations shake the ground above. Usually the vibrations are minute and hardly detectable, but sometimes they shatter buildings and cause widespread destruction and death. These vibrations are known as earthquakes. The point at which an earthquake occurs is called the focus. This is usually somewhere along a deep fault. The point on the earth's surface immediately above the focus, where most, if any, damage is done, is called the epicenter. There tends to be less and less damage farther away from the epicenter.

An earthquake produces a number of different shock waves. The first are the P waves. These produce a back-and-forth pushing action. The second are the S waves. They produce a side-to-side shaking action. The third

The Anchorage, Alaska, earthquake in 1964 was caused by plate movement in the Aleutian island destructive plate margin.

are the L waves. These are the long waves that travel along the surface and cause the actual damage. The waves can be picked up by sensitive instruments called seismographs. Scientists can then use them to calculate the strength of an earthquake and where it actually occurred.

Because we know where the main regions of plate activity are, we know where earthquakes are most likely to occur. Areas within these zones may not have suffered an earthquake for a number of years. But people living there should not be unconcerned. The stresses are building up in these areas all the time. If the pressures are not released by a number of small, harmless tremors, they will certainly be released by a few catastrophic earthquakes.

A

Light waves enter

Light source

B

A An optical fiber is glued to a rock. Another optical fiber of the same length is not glued to the rock. Light waves are emitted in phase to give a brilliant light.
B When the rock is stressed, light waves are emitted out of phase. They cancel each other out, so no light appears.

Can we predict an earthquake?

Unfortunately, we cannot yet make predictions. Many attempts have been made to devise prediction systems, but often they have failed to predict disastrous earthquakes. Most such schemes are based on measuring gradual deformations in the rocks of earthquake-prone regions.

A promising new method lies in fiber optics. A thin hair made of glass will transmit light along its length. This ability to transmit light changes if the hair is subjected to stress. A fiber optic hair glued to a rock will be stressed if that rock is stressed, so potential earthquake forces can be detected by the amount of light coming through.

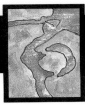

THE HOT PLUMBING

Anyone who needs convincing that the earth is an active, evolving body needs only to look at an active volcano. Steam and gases belch out of a vent in the ground. Ash and dust are blasted explosively into the atmosphere. Molten rock oozes upward from somewhere deep below our feet. It is an awesome sight. But for all its majestic splendor, a volcano is merely a side issue. It is a byproduct of the movement of the earth's plates.

Geologists recognize two main types of volcano. They are different in their shapes, their eruptions, the kind of stony material they produce, and where they occur.

GENTLE GIANTS

The first kind are the basaltic types. Their lava hardens into a fine-grained rock called basalt. These volcanoes erupt quietly, producing large volumes of runny, black lava that flows over large areas to produce broad, low volcanoes. These are found at constructive plate margins where new material is welling up from beneath the crust to form the new plates. Most basaltic volcanoes are located at the bottom of the ocean.

However, there is one place on the earth's surface where the constructive margin produces an oceanic ridge that rises above sea level. The result is a broad island made up entirely of these shield volcanoes and flat lava flows. This island is a wilderness of broken lava surfaces, cindery conical mountains, and deserts of black sand. This is Iceland.

Basaltic volcanoes can also be found in the middle of the ocean away from any constructive plate margin. Hawaii is a chain of islands made of shield volcanoes. They may result from a "hot spot" beneath the earth's crust. At a "hot spot," the activity in the mantle is strong. Hot material is punched up to the surface.

Basaltic volcanoes, like those on Hawaii, throw up a runny kind of lava in spectacular fire fountains. This lava can flow for many kilometers and build up a very low, shieldlike volcano on a foundation of thick masses of earlier lava flows.

Eruption starts as fire fountains along a crack then becomes a one-vent eruption. Lava surface is wrinkled

Fire fountain eruption Continuous spray of molten material

Broad, low shield volcano

Frequently much of the cone is blown away in an explosive eruption

Thick cauliflower clouds of ash and dust

Lava is thicker and slower than basaltic type. Forms steep-sided volcano

Andesitic volcanoes, like Mount Saint Helens in the Coast Ranges of North America, are made of a very stiff lava forced up through crumpled continental rocks. They erupt very violently. Their explosions can send hot clouds of ash and dust for great distances, engulfing the surrounding countryside.

THE KILLERS

The other type of volcano, the andesitic volcano, is different. Andesitic lava is much thicker and stiffer than basaltic lava. It forms steep-sided volcanoes because the thick lava can flow only a short distance before it solidifies. Often the lava hardens before it can pour out of the volcanic vent. When this happens, the vent is blocked. The pressure builds up beneath. This pressure can be released only by a great explosion that blasts away the solid plug. Usually, a large part of the volcanic mountain is also blasted away. A white-hot blast of ash and gas can engulf the surrounding countryside and destroy everything in its path. This is what happened at Mount Saint Helens in 1980 and at Mount Vesuvius in 69 A.D.

Andesitic volcanoes usually occur on the continents at destructive plate margins. They also erupt at sea where two oceanic plates collide. Basaltic lava is derived from new material coming up from the mantle and forming new plates. Andesitic lava is made up of plate material melted by the friction of one plate crunching down beneath the other. As a result, there is more of the chemical silica in the lava. The silica makes the lava stiffer and more difficult to melt. The lava is usually brown or gray.

The gentle eruptions of basaltic volcanoes are regarded as tourist attractions. Andesitic volcanoes, on the other hand, are treated with fear and a great deal of respect.

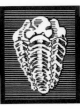
When a steel ship is built, its navigation compasses do not work properly for a few months. Why should this be?

To find out, we must first look at how a compass works. The earth has a magnetic field. In other words, it acts like a huge magnet. Like other magnets, its magnetism is strongest at each end, at the North and South poles. One of the properties of a magnet is that it will attract one pole of another magnet and repel that magnet's other pole. Hence a compass needle, which is itself a little magnet, will turn so that one of its poles will point to the earth's North Pole and the other will turn away from it.

What does this have to do with a newly built ship? The connection is that when a piece of iron or steel is hammered, the particles that form it are momentarily loosened. Because these particles are little magnets, they will realign themselves to point toward and away from the earth's North and South poles. The whole of the piece of iron or steel will then become a magnet itself. It is the same with a ship under construction on a slipway. After months and years of hammering, welding, and riveting, the ship becomes one enormous magnet. The magnet in its navigation compass will then be so confused by the surrounding magnetism that it will not be able to point to the earth's North Pole. After a few months at sea, however, the new ship has had such a battering by the waves that it loses all this magnetism. The compass can then work without trouble.

The same thing happens with rocks. When a rock forms, any magnetic particles in it will

The magnetic particles trapped in bricks made in ancient Egypt show that the earth's magnetic field has changed in the mere 3,000 years since their manufacture.

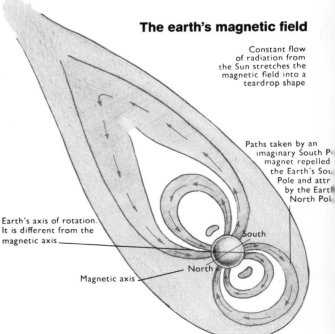

The earth's magnetic field

Constant flow of radiation from the Sun stretches the magnetic field into a teardrop shape

Paths taken by an imaginary South P magnet repelled the Earth's Sou Pole and attr by the Eart North Pol

Earth's axis of rotation. It is different from the magnetic axis

Magnetic axis

South

North

align themselves with the earth's magnetic field. The particles will be locked in that position. It does not matter whether the rocks hardened from lava or from a heap of sand. Now, millions of years later, geologists can study these rocks and find their magnetic alignment. They have discovered that the magnetic particles do not point to the earth's poles as they are today. Either the earth's poles have moved since the rocks formed or the rocks themselves have moved. It is more likely that the rocks, and the continents on which they lie, have shifted. Geologists can use this magnetic information to work out how the continents have been moving throughout time.

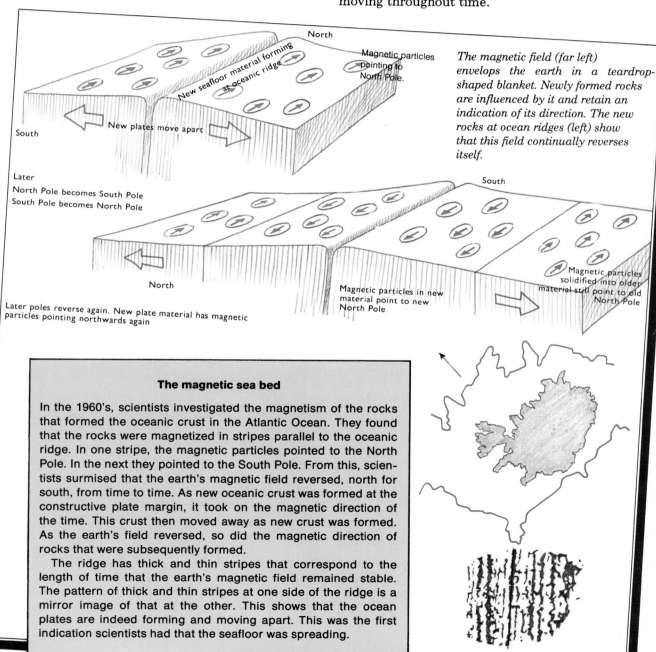

North

New seafloor material forming at oceanic ridge

Magnetic particles pointing to North Pole.

The magnetic field (far left) envelops the earth in a teardrop-shaped blanket. Newly formed rocks are influenced by it and retain an indication of its direction. The new rocks at ocean ridges (left) show that this field continually reverses itself.

South

New plates move apart

Later
North Pole becomes South Pole
South Pole becomes North Pole

South

North

Magnetic particles in new material point to new North Pole

Magnetic particles solidified into older material still point to old North Pole

Later poles reverse again. New plate material has magnetic particles pointing northwards again

The magnetic sea bed

In the 1960's, scientists investigated the magnetism of the rocks that formed the oceanic crust in the Atlantic Ocean. They found that the rocks were magnetized in stripes parallel to the oceanic ridge. In one stripe, the magnetic particles pointed to the North Pole. In the next they pointed to the South Pole. From this, scientists surmised that the earth's magnetic field reversed, north for south, from time to time. As new oceanic crust was formed at the constructive plate margin, it took on the magnetic direction of the time. This crust then moved away as new crust was formed. As the earth's field reversed, so did the magnetic direction of rocks that were subsequently formed.

The ridge has thick and thin stripes that correspond to the length of time that the earth's magnetic field remained stable. The pattern of thick and thin stripes at one side of the ridge is a mirror image of that at the other. This shows that the ocean plates are indeed forming and moving apart. This was the first indication scientists had that the seafloor was spreading.

ROCK-FORMING MINERALS

THE BUILDING BRICKS OF ROCKS

If you look at almost any rock through a hand lens or a microscope, you will see it is formed from a mass of small fragments. These small fragments are pieces of chemical substances that we call minerals.

A rock is usually made up of several different minerals. There is a different set of minerals in each type of rock. Hundreds of different minerals exist. Each one has a different chemical composition. However, there are only a dozen or so that occur time and time again in the rocks of the earth's crust.

One of the most common chemical substances in the earth is silica. This is made up of the elements silicon and oxygen. Ordinary glass is made up of almost pure silica. Most minerals contain silica in their chemical composition. The mineral quartz is pure silica.

The common metals of the earth's crust are iron, magnesium, and aluminum. The bulk of the minerals in most rocks, therefore, contain iron, magnesium, or aluminum combined with silica. These are called silicates. An example of olivine, which is a silicate mineral containing both iron and magnesium.

Another common element is sulfur. Hence, another common group of minerals is the sulfate group. Minerals in this group consist of a metal combined with sulfer and oxygen. An example is gypsum, a magnesium sulfate, which gives us plaster of Paris.

The different minerals form in geometrically shaped solids called crystals.

When we hear the word crystal, we immediately think of the magnificent specimens that we see behind glass in mineral collections and museums. These are usually brightly colored, have shiny faces and sharp edges, and look very beautiful. These, however, are very unusual. They are the natural shapes into which that particular mineral will grow, but only if it has room to grow properly. When rocks form, the different minerals are growing together and pressing in on one another. As a result, they rarely form such good shapes. They

When a thin section of a rock is examined through a microscope, its individual minerals can be seen. In this section of basalt (above), the large crystals of augite must have formed first, because they are large and have quite good crystal shapes. The later-formed mass of feldspar and mica then solidified in a mass of tiny crystals in between. Well-shaped crystals, like the quartz (top right), can form only in cavities.

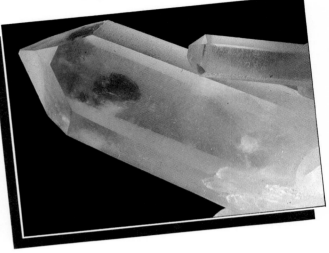

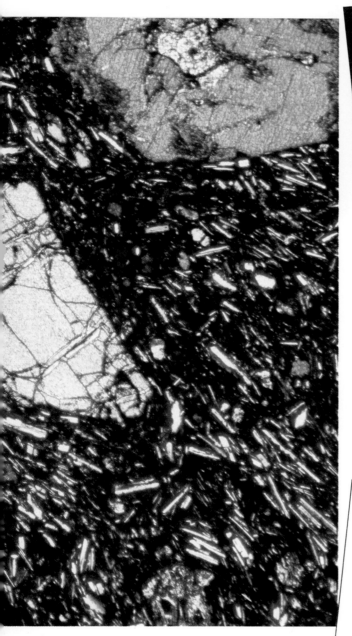

can grow only into spaces left between the minerals that crystallized earlier. So crystals become interlocked. Perfect crystal shapes develop only where the mineral is forming in a cavity in the rock or in a liquid substance.

Because iron and magnesium, and many other metals, are extremely common in the minerals of the earth's crust, we might think that most rocks are potentially valuable storehouses of these metals. But, this is not true. When a metal is chemically combined with silica (as in most common minerals), it is extremely difficult and expensive to extract.

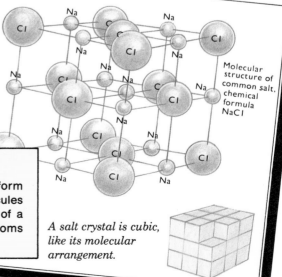

Molecular structure of common salt, chemical formula NaCl

A salt crystal is cubic, like its molecular arrangement.

The shapes of minerals

The atoms of a substance link together in a certain way to form a molecule of that substance. To form a crystal, the molecules build up by repeating their basic shape. Thus the shape of a crystal of a mineral depends on the arrangement of the atoms in the molecule.

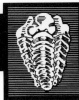
THE EARTH'S RICHES CONCENTRATED

In 1848 gold was discovered in California. All over the world, people sold their possessions and sailed to the west coast of the United States in the hope of making their fortune. The great American gold rush had started.

Why was there gold in "them thar hills"? Gold is indeed a very valuable commodity, but it is found to some extent in most of the rocks of the earth's crust. It is estimated that there are even six million tons of gold dissolved in the ocean. That is a hundred times more gold than is found in banks and treasuries around the world. However, gold concentration in common rocks and in the ocean waters is so small that it is not worthwhile to extract it. Once in a while, however, easily workable deposits of gold do occur. A rock that contains a little bit more gold than usual may be exposed in a cliff face, but it is still not worth the expense of mining. However, if this rock is eroded by the wind and the weather, and the broken fragments are washed down streams and rivers, the gold may become more concentrated. Gold is one of the heaviest metals. A stream cannot carry gold particles as far as it can carry other mineral debris. The gold collects in the stream beds and on sandbanks. There it can be easily washed out and gathered by prospectors and mining companies.

The gold in this example is known as "native metal." That means that the naturally formed mineral contains the metal and nothing else. So, once the mineral is collected, it does not need to be extracted from its chemical compound. Silver is also found as native metal.

Some other useful metals, such as copper and zinc, can form native ore minerals. Usually they are combined with other elements. When they are present as oxide (combined with oxygen) or as sulfate (combined with sulfur and oxygen), they are still regarded as ore minerals. The metal is quite easy to extract from the mineral after the mineral has been mined.

These minerals form most often in structures that the miners call veins. When hot molten

rock from deep within the earth is forced into the rocks of the crust, the water in the nearby rocks is heated. This hot water may dissolve minerals from the hot molten rock. Then it works its way through cracks and faults, depositing these minerals as it cools. That is why there are often long streaks of ore minerals in the rocks surrounding granites. The granites were formed from molten material that solidified and cooled millions of years ago.

Sometimes the ore minerals collect in the cooling mass itself. When the molten rock solidifies to form a solid rock like granite, some minerals solidify before others. An ore mineral may form early. Then its crystals may sink through the molten mass and gather at the base. Many big nickel mines in Canada are excavated into hard rock masses like these to extract the metal-rich seams.

The twisted crystals of native silver (left) are often found along the edges of silver sulfide veins. The iron oxide mineral hematite (above), sometimes called kidney ore because of its appearance, occurs where the iron in a sedimentary rock has been collected by groundwater. Its iron content is about 70 percent.

The Cornish tin mines of western England are sunk around the edges of huge masses of granite. Here the tin lies in veins that formed from hot fluids given off as the granite cooled.

BORN IN FIRE

How did rocks form? That question has fascinated scientists since the beginning of civilization. We now know that there are three main processes that produce the rocks of the earth's crust. Presumably, the crusts of the other solid planets formed this way as well. These processes give rise to three distinct types of rock.

The first of these is igneous rock. It was formed as molten, rocky material hardened. This process is similar to the process of molten steel and slag pouring from a furnace and hardens into solid masses as they cool or of liquid water freezing to solid ice as the temperature drops.

The most obvious occurrence of igneous rock is from a volcano. Molten lava flows out of an erupting volcano and solidifies into wrinkled masses or jagged lumps. The rock that forms is an igneous rock. Geologists call this an *extrusive* igneous rock because it is extruded from, or forced out of, the ground.

The two different types of volcanoes produce two different extrusive igneous rocks. Heavy, black basalt is extruded from shield volcanoes. Pale-colored, silica-rich andesite forms from the lavas of destructive plate margin volcanoes.

This process of solidification can also take place underground. Molten material from deep in the earth may be forced into the rocks of the crust. It thrusts its way through cracks, melting and absorbing the crustal rocks as it travels through them. It finally solidifies in a mass long before reaching the surface. Such a mass may never appear at the surface. If it does, it will not be until millions of years later, after all the overlying rocks have been worn away. Such a deep-seated rock is known as an *intrusive* igneous rock.

Again different types of rock form, depending on the composition of the original liquid. A liquid low in silica, like that which produces the

Igneous fluids seep through cracks and weaknesses, and solidify into strangely-shaped rock-masses underground. These form distinctive landscape features once the overlying rocks are eroded.

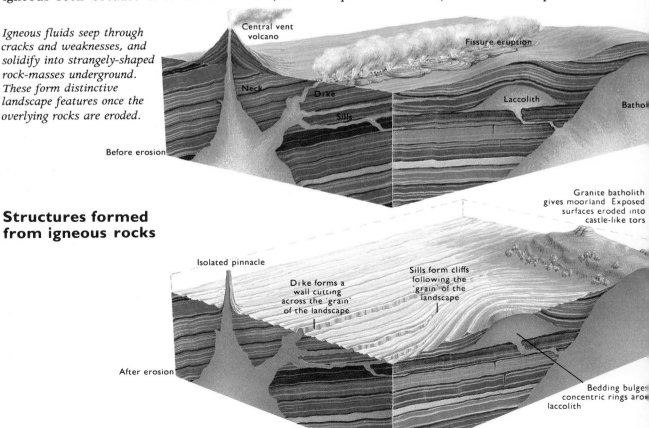

Structures formed from igneous rocks

Basalt (above) cools quickly as it flows from a volcano. It forms a fine-grained rock.

Coarse-grained rock like granite (below) is formed by slow cooling underground.

basalt on the surface, will form a dark rock called gabbro. A silica-rich liquid will form the light-colored rock that we call granite. Granite is the intrusive equivalent of andesite.

Geologists can easily tell whether an igneous rock is extrusive or intrusive. An extrusive igneous rock cools quickly when it is exposed to air, so the mineral crystals do not have time to grow very large. This produces a rock with a very fine grain. The magma of an intrusive rock cools very slowly underground, so the crystals can grow to quite a size to form a coarse-grained rock.

Igneous structures

Intrusive igneous rocks can form a number of different structures. The largest is the batholith, in which an enormous volume of rock solidifies deep beneath the earth's surface. There are also many smaller structures, such as dikes, sills, necks, and laccoliths. Dikes are wall-like structures that form where the magma is forced upward through vertical cracks in the surrounding rocks. Horizontal structures called sills develop where the liquid has worked its way between the different layers, or beds, of the surrounding rock. A neck is a cylindrical structure punched upward, usually leading to a volcano. A laccolith forms as a small reservoir of igneous material bulges into the rocks above. Once these structures have solidified and the surrounding rocks have worn away, the igneous rocks may form distinctive landscape features.

Devil's Tower in Wyoming (above) is a vertical neck of igneous rock. The soft rocks of the surrounding area have been worn away, leaving the tower isolated.

27

SEDIMENTARY ROCKS

BORN IN WATER

The second type of rock is sedimentary rock. This type of rock is formed from sediments. Take a look at the sand on a beach, the mud in a puddle, the silt in a river bed. These are all sediments. They may eventually turn into stone. When they do, they will become sedimentary rocks. There are three ways in which a sediment can accumulate, producing three different kinds of sedimentary rock.

Rocks at the earth's surface crumble away when they are exposed to weather and air. The fragments are washed away in rivers or blown away by wind and deposited in the sea or in lakes or on beaches. These sediments are made up of clastic fragments and produce *clastic* sedimentary rocks. Coarse clastic fragments produce shingle. When these fragments are cemented together, they form the rock conglomerate. Medium-grained clastic sediments are sands, which eventually produce sandstone. Fine material is mud, which gives mudstone or shale.

Seawater has many different salts dissolved in it. So does the water in some lakes. If the water evaporates, the salts may fall out of solution and accumulate as layers on the sea bed or lake bed. These layers may eventually form

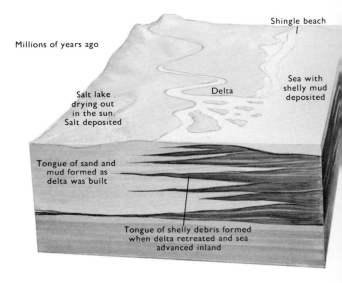

Millions of years ago

Shingle beach

Salt lake drying out in the sun. Salt deposited

Delta

Sea with shelly mud deposited

Tongue of sand and mud formed as delta was built

Tongue of shelly debris formed when delta retreated and sea advanced inland

chemical sedimentary rocks. Rock salt and certain kinds of limestones are formed this way.

Finally, the remains of plants and animals may produce a third type of sedimentary rock. The most familiar example is coal. Masses upon masses of woody material built up in the shallow waters of a swamp. They were eventually buried and turned to rock. Many limestones are made up almost entirely of the shells of ancient sea creatures. The shells accumulated on an old sea bed or were washed up on a beach. These limestones are known as *biogenic* sedimentary rocks.

How do these loose sediments become hard rock? Two processes are involved. A sand bank, a bed of limy mud, or a heap of broken shells may be buried by more sediments deposited on top of it. The weight of the overlying sediments becomes so great that the particles of sand or mud or shells are crushed together. Air spaces are squeezed out. Then groundwater may filter through the sediments and deposit minerals in any spaces that are left between the particles. This cements them together. This is the same process as cementing sand and gravel together to make concrete.

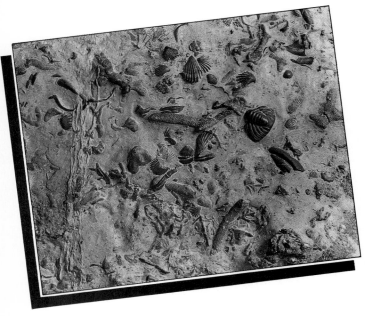

Origin of sedimentary rocks

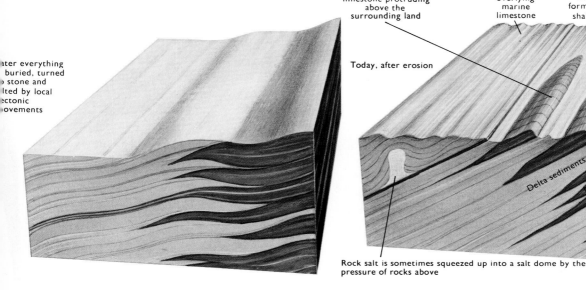

ter everything
buried, turned
stone and
lted by local
ctonic
ovements

Thick, resistant
beds of marine
limestone protruding
above the
surrounding land

Conglomerate
overlying
marine
limestone

Sandstone
and shale interbedded.
Resistant sandstone
forms shelves, the soft
shale is eroded away

Today, after erosion

Delta sediments

Marine sediments

Rock salt is sometimes squeezed up into a salt dome by the
pressure of rocks above

*Sediments can be layers of sand and rubble brought down
by rivers and washed up by the waves, salts deposited
from evaporating seas and lakes, or masses of shells and
other materials produced by living things (left). Once
compacted and cemented, these become sedimentary rocks
(center). When they outcrop at the surface they do so
as a series of beds. The layered nature of the original
sediments (right) shows clearly.*

*Shelly limestone (far left) is a biogenic rock. We can still
see the shells that formed the original sediment.
Conglomerate (left) is a clastic sedimentary rock. It
is obviously made of broken fragments.*

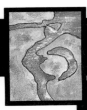

METAMORPHIC ROCKS

NEW ROCKS FROM OLD

A third type of rock is formed in a completely different way. Its raw material is not a hot mass of liquid from deep below the surface or deposits of loose sand from the crumbling debris of exposed rocks. Instead, it is formed directly from igneous or sedimentary rocks that are already in existence. This is metamorphic rock.

In the depths of fold mountain chains, the crushing pressure of the moving plates tortures and twists the rocks of the crust and crushes them into fantastic structures. The pressures and the temperatures are so great that the rocks are cooked and altered beyond recognition. They are chemically broken down and reformed into metamorphic rocks.

There are two types of metamorphic rocks. In the first, pressure, rather than heat, changes the rock. Pressure produces what geologists call *regional* metamorphic rocks. Great areas of the earth's crust are altered in this way. The chemical composition of a metamorphic rock is usually the same as that of the rock that was altered. However, a different set of minerals have grown in it. If shale is subjected to weak pressure, the minerals recrystallize along the direction of the forces. This produces slate, which splits easily along lines of weakness. Greater pressures will turn the same rock into schist. In schist the minerals crystallize in bands. The flaky mineral mica crystallizes with its flat surfaces at right angles to the direction of stress. Schist also splits easily along the shiny mica bands. Even greater pressure will cause the rock to recrystallize into gneiss. Gneiss has distinct contorted layers of the new minerals.

As a rule, we expect to find metamorphic rocks at the heart of a continent. They are overlain by sedimentary rocks. In new or old mountain areas, igneous rocks may be found at the surface.

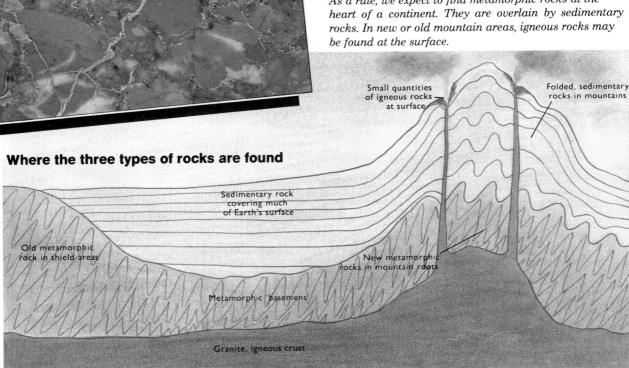

Where the three types of rocks are found

Small quantities of igneous rocks at surface

Folded, sedimentary rocks in mountains

Sedimentary rock covering much of Earth's surface

Old metamorphic rock in shield areas

New metamorphic rocks in mountain roots

Metamorphic basement

Granite, igneous crust

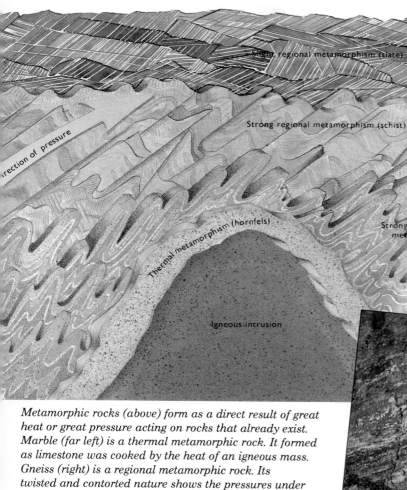

Slight regional metamorphism (slate)

Strong regional metamorphism (schist)

Direction of pressure

Thermal metamorphism (hornfels)

Strong regional and thermal metamorphism (gneiss)

Igneous intrusion

Metamorphic rocks (above) form as a direct result of great heat or great pressure acting on rocks that already exist. Marble (far left) is a thermal metamorphic rock. It formed as limestone was cooked by the heat of an igneous mass. Gneiss (right) is a regional metamorphic rock. Its twisted and contorted nature shows the pressures under which it formed in the heart of a mountain chain.

The second kind of metamorphic rock is produced by the action of heat. The rock surrounding a hot igneous intrusion is cooked by the heat of the liquid. These high temperatures cause the minerals to recrystallize, producing *thermal* metamorphic rocks. Unlike regional metamorphic rocks, these tend to have no bands or layers. They are dense and lumpy and look similar to igneous rocks. However, they can contain minerals unique to thermal metamorphic rock.

The important thing about all of these rocks is that the original rock did not melt while it was being changed. If that had happened, the result would be an igneous rock, not a metamorphic rock. All the changes involved in metamorphism take place when the rock is solid.

The centers of all the continents consist of very old metamorphic rocks. The mountains in which they formed have long since been eroded away. Only these hard, ancient cores remain. In the surrounding regions, the sedimentary rocks are the most common at the earth's surface. Below the surface, it is the igneous rocks that make up the greatest proportion of the earth's crust.

THE BIRTHDAYS OF THE AGING EARTH

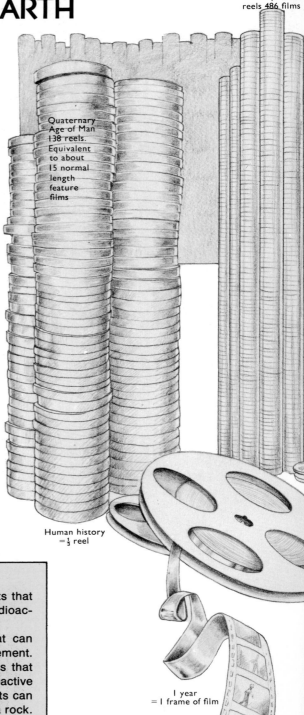

Tertiary 4,375 reels 486 films

Quaternary Age of Man 138 reels. Equivalent to about 15 normal length feature films

Human history = $\frac{1}{3}$ reel

1 year = 1 frame of film

The earth started to form about 4.5 thousand million years ago. The oldest rocks are 3.8 thousand million years old. The oldest good fossils are 590 million years old. Humans appeared 2 million years ago.

These are the figures, but can you visualize such a huge time scale? Geological time is a very difficult concept. The great lengths involved are almost impossible to understand. We are used to dealing with events in years. The earliest known civilizations started only about 5 thousand years ago.

Let us look at it in another way.

A movie film runs at 24 frames per second. That means that every second you are watching the film, 24 pictures are flashed onto the screen. Let us imagine that the earth's history is recorded on a film. Each year is recorded on a single frame. The whole life of a person would flash by in about three seconds. The human history that we learn at school would last only about three minutes. Humans would have been in existence for less than a day. Animals that left fossils would have been in existence for about ten months, although simple living things would have been around for much longer than that. The age of the oldest rocks would be about five years. The length of time that would take us to the origin of the earth would be over six years. This would be an amazingly long movie!

How old is a rock?

How are scientists able to put dates on geological events that happened millions of years ago? The secret lies in the radioactive isotopes of some elements.

A radioactive isotope is an atom of an element that can change spontaneously into an atom of a different element. Energy is released during this change. It is this process that produces power in an atomic power station. Every radioactive isotope changes, or decays, at a particular rate. Scientists can measure the amount of a radioactive isotope present in a rock. They then compare it with the amount of its daughter element. The daughter element is the substance into which it changes. These measurements tell how long the original isotope has been there. Thus scientists can fix a date for the formation of that rock.

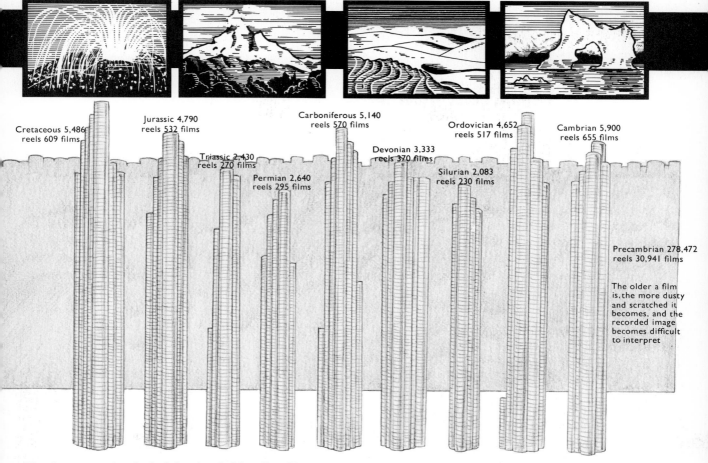

Cretaceous 5,486 reels 609 films

Jurassic 4,790 reels 532 films

Triassic 2,430 reels 270 films

Permian 2,640 reels 295 films

Carboniferous 5,140 reels 570 films

Devonian 3,333 reels 370 films

Silurian 2,083 reels 230 films

Ordovician 4,652 reels 517 films

Cambrian 5,900 reels 655 films

Precambrian 278,472 reels 30,941 films

The older a film is, the more dusty and scratched it becomes, and the recorded image becomes difficult to interpret

The sheer span of geological time is mind-boggling. If each year were recorded on a single frame of movie film, the entire film of the history of the world would take over six years to run.

The conventional geological column (below) has the oldest rock sequences and time divisions at the bottom. The youngest are at the top.

To make these time spans easier to understand, geologists do not talk about them in terms of years or millions of years. Instead, they divide geological time into periods. There are about a dozen different periods, as shown on the chart. The periods are grouped together to form different epochs. Because the boundaries between the periods are based on the changes of fossils formed at these times, the periods apply only to the last 590 million years. Before that, the history of life is pretty vague.

We can plot the history of life as it evolved during these periods. In the Cambrian period, animals with hard shells and skeletons appeared. In the Silurian period there were the first fish. Plants and animals left the sea and colonized the land in the Devonian period. The Carboniferous period was the time of the coal forests. The dinosaurs lived between the Triassic and the Cretaceous periods. During the Cenozoic period, the mammals developed into the important group that they are today. The Quaternary covers the Ice Age and the Age of Man.

Geological column

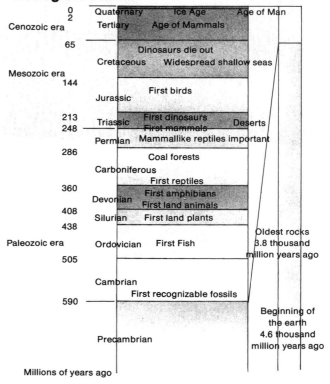

Cenozoic era	0	Quaternary	Ice Age	Age of Man
	2	Tertiary	Age of Mammals
	65		Dinosaurs die out
		Cretaceous	Widespread shallow seas
Mesozoic era	144		
		Jurassic	First birds
	213	Triassic	First dinosaurs
	248		First mammals	Deserts
		Permian	Mammallike reptiles important
	286		Coal forests
		Carboniferous	
	360		First reptiles
		Devonian	First amphibians
	408		First land animals
		Silurian	First land plants
	438		
Paleozoic era		Ordovician	First Fish
	505		
		Cambrian	
	590		First recognizable fossils
		Precambrian	

Oldest rocks 3.8 thousand million years ago

Beginning of the earth 4.6 thousand million years ago

Millions of years ago

33

FOSSILS

GEOLOGY'S MAUSOLEUM

In books describing life in the prehistoric world, we see pictures of dinosaurs tearing at one another among strange plants. Pterosaurs wheel and screech overhead. The landscapes are steamy, damp, green coal forests. There are many illustrations of what the sea bed was like millions of years ago. Restorations have been made of mammoth herds moving across the Ice Age wilderness. Sometimes these pictures are rather fanciful. However, all of them are based, to some extent, on what scientists know of life that existed in the distant past.

How do scientists know these things? They have never seen a dinosaur on the rampage, or hacked their way through a coal forest, or swum in warm trilobite-infested lagoons, or shivered on the edge of an Ice Age glacier.

They know because pieces of shell, bone, or wood are often found preserved in sedimentary rocks. From these fragments, scientists can build up a picture of what life was like in the past. These fragments are called fossils.

Only very rarely does a fossil consist of the entire animal or plant. Sometimes an insect has been embedded whole in sticky tree resin. The resin hardens to become amber. A few mammoths have been preserved in frozen mud. More often, the soft parts soon decay. Only the hard parts of the organism are fossilized. For example, sharks' teeth are found in Cenozoic clays. The bones of saber-toothed tigers have been found in natural tar pits in California.

It is usual for the substance of the fossil to have been altered in some way. Often the wood of an ancient tree has been replaced by the mineral silica. This results in an exact replica of the tissues in the tree but in a completely different substance. This is how petrified wood is formed. Under other conditions, the organic material of a fern leaf can decay to leave only a thin film of carbon in the shape of the leaf.

Cast of brachiopod shellfish, Platystrophia.

Fern Neuropteris *preserved as a carbon film.*

A petrified trunk of the oak tree, Quercus.

Unaltered tooth of the shark, Carcharodon.

Fossils as environmental indicators

Some animals can live only under particular environmental conditions. The fossil of such an animal in a rock may show that the rock formed under those conditions. Such a fossil is called a *facies* fossil. This is useful to the oil geologist, for example, who is looking for oil-producing rocks that formed only in an oxygen-deficient environment.

Sometimes a plant or animal dissolves away entirely, leaving a hole in the rock in its exact shape. This kind of fossil is called a mold. The mold may later be filled with minerals deposited from groundwater. This process gives a mineral mass called a cast. The exact shape of the original plant or animal is reproduced.

Often there is no sign of the original organism at all, just traces. Ancient worm tunnels in sandstone or reptile footprints in mud are examples of these trace fossils.

Most often many fossils are found in one place. This indicates the range of animals and plants that lived in a particular area at a particular time.

The footprint of a dinosaur. This is a trace fossil.

Fossil timekeepers

Animals that live in all the seas of the world at a particular time can produce *index* fossils. Geologists who find an index fossil in a rock can date that rock if they know when the animal lived.

SEDIMENTARY STRUCTURES

FOOTPRINTS IN THE SANDS OF TIME

Scientists can use fossils to tell them about the animal and plant life that existed in the past. But there is other evidence they can use to show what kind of world these creatures inhabited.

For an organism to become fossilized, it must be buried in sediment quite quickly after death before it rots away. Therefore only creatures that live near areas of sediment accumulation are likely to become fossilized. A land-living plant or animal will be fossilized only if it falls into a river and is buried in river sands or if it is washed to the sea and buried in mud.

Sediments can sometimes preserve traces of the conditions in which an organism lived.

If you visit a beach at low tide, you can see the ripple marks in the sand. This is where the waves have washed back and forth, sorting out the sand particles as they go. Ripples such as these are often found preserved in beds of sandstone dating from millions of years ago. When we find such beds, we can tell that they were laid down in shallow water. The ripples show that waves had been moving the sand grains.

Where a muddy pool dries up in the sun, the mud shrinks and cracks. These cracks can be preserved in mudstone. When mud cracks are found, scientists can tell that the original mudstone was laid down in pools that dried out.

Another sign of drying out is the shapes of salt crystals. Seawater evaporated, leaving the salt behind. The salt was later dissolved. The next layer of mud laid down filled the hollows left and produced a series of structures in the exact shape of the salt crystals. Rain falling on mud makes pit and splashes. These are sometimes preserved in sedimentary rock.

These features are all signs of static, shallow water, or of pools drying up. Water currents leave different traces behind. A river current deposits sand in characteristic S-shaped beds in a delta or an estuary. As the river course shifts, more S-shaped beds are deposited over the first. A succession of curved features called current bedding is built up. Sand dunes in a desert can form curved structures, but on a much larger scale. Sandstones that have formed in a desert often show this dune bedding.

Deep-sea currents give different structures. As a current carries sand, silt, and stones along, the heaviest material settles first as the current slackens. Then, as the current slackens even more, the less heavy material settles out. Finally the lightest and finest material is laid down. The result is a graded bed. Coarse fragments are found at the base of the bed and finer pieces farther up.

These deep-sea currents can erode as well as deposit material. A sudden current sweeping across the seafloor can scoop out hollows in the sediment. Shells and other debris can bounce across the ground, leaving holes and marks in the mud. All of these may be preserved in the final sedimentary rock as proof of the conditions that existed at the time the original sediments were laid down.

Sole marks (right) were formed when fierce currents washed away part of the sediment of the sea bed. They were preserved when the bed became a sedimentary rock. Fossil ripple marks (far right) show where a sediment was laid down in shallow water. The cross bedding in desert sandstone (inset right) was formed by winds blowing the sand into dunes.

THE CRUMBLING EARTH SURFACE

The highest mountains of the world are among the youngest features on our planet's surface. The great Himalayan mountain chain, 1,500 miles (2,400 kilometers) long and up to 29,029 feet (8,848 meters) high, started to rise only some 50 million years ago. This is about three weeks ago in our six-year-long movie film. (see *Geological Time — The Birthdays of An Aging Earth*). The Andes, 5,500 miles (8,900 kilometers) long and 22,831 (6,959 meters) high, are still rising. Older mountain chains, such as the Urals and the Scottish Highlands are much lower. They are 6,214 feet (1,894 meters) and 4,406 feet (1,343 meters) high, respectively.

Yet, once upon a time, these old mountain ranges were as high and as rugged as the greatest mountain chains of today. What has happened to them since?

The simple answer is that they have eroded in the rain. Not just rain, however, but wind, snow, frost, and all the other weather conditions have combined to grind down the hills and mountains that were once pushed upward by the action of plate tectonics. It is as if there is a particular level above which no landscape is allowed to rise before the forces of nature conspire to wear it down again.

The process is called weathering. Geologists recognize two types — chemical weathering and physical weathering.

CHEMICAL WEATHERING

Rainwater is rarely pure. Nowadays, moisture in the air can dissolve chemicals from factory smoke and cause "acid rain" to fall in distant places, harming wildlife. This can happen in nature, too.

Carbon dioxide, one of the most common gases in the air, can dissolve in rainwater to make a weak carbonic acid. This acid may then react with minerals in the rocks when it falls as rain. The most obvious result is the weathering of limestone. Limestone is made up almost entirely of the mineral calcite, which is particularly susceptible to acid attack. Whole caverns and gorges can be dissolved out of limestone areas. The calcite is converted into soluble calcium bicarbonate, which is carried away by streams and rivers.

Rainwater also effects granite. Granite consists mostly of the tough minerals quartz and mica and large crystals of the weaker mineral feldspar. The feldspar breaks down when exposed to rain. As it disintegrates, the crystals of quartz and mica work loose and are washed away. The feldspar, in this process, becomes china clay (kaolin). This is a whitish clay used to make porcelain. That is why, in granite areas, there are often china clay mines, which exploit the new deposits of clay. Good white beaches are also found. These are made up of quartz worked loose from the granite.

The effects of chemical weathering are well seen in limestone areas. The weak acid of rainwater reacts with the calcite of the limestone, dissolving it and forming gullies and gorges (far left).

PHYSICAL WEATHERING

Rainwater may seep into cracks and pores in a rock. Then, in cold weather, the water freezes and expands, forcing the crack open farther. This process is repeated until pieces of the rock break away. The accumulations of rocks and other debris seen in hilly areas are the results of this "frost-wedging." This is an example of physical weathering.

A desert is the kind of environment in which most physical weathering occurs. With no moisture, the soil particles cannot hold together. The wind then hurls the sand grains against the rocks, wearing the rocks down by constant sandblasting.

All these effects turn solid rock into broken debris. The debris is then transported and deposited as a sediment. This is the raw material of clastic sedimentary rock.

Physical weathering is very noticeable in cold areas. Repeated freezing and thawing shatter hillsides into scree slopes (center). Deserts also show noticeable effects of physical weathering. The fierce desert wind blasts sand against exposed rocks and wears them away (right).

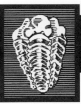
THE THREE AGES OF RIVERS

The lives of human beings are sometimes seen as consisting of three stages. When we are young, we are full of energy. We run around all the time. Then we grow up. That is when the work gets done. We are mature enough to make something of our lives. Finally we reach old age. Everything slows down for us and we can relax. Geologists see the life of a river in these three stages as well.

A youthful river flows through mountainous areas. It is a rushing stream, tumbling off hillsides as waterfalls and rapids. Rocks broken from the banks and stream beds are washed out and tumbled along. They loosen other rocks and break down still further. The speed and violence of the water's movement erode steep V-shaped valleys.

Then comes the mature stage. The river increases its volume. It flows sedately through broad valleys. It carries much of the material eroded from the mountain gorges. But as the river flows more slowly, it deposits some of the larger particles of rock. Sand banks and sand spits are built up. There are no waterfalls and few rapids in the mature stage of a river. All the irregularities in the river bed have been smoothed out.

When a river reaches old age, it does not run in a valley at all. Instead, it runs across a wide, flat floodplain. No downward erosion takes place because the river flows so sluggishly. It winds across the plain in broad loops called meanders. From time to time the river floods. It overflows its banks and pours muddy water over the surrounding area. At these times, sand and mud are deposited on the banks. Barriers called levees are built up. Sometimes the river between the levees is higher than the surrounding plain.

A youthful river (above) is vigorous. It splashes and falls in ravines and waterfalls, eroding a deep gully downward through the mountains. At the end of its life the river is slow and wandering (left). It has no strength left. It moves slowly across the open plain, depositing mud and sand as it goes and finally emptying into the sea.

The course of the river across its floodplain is not constant. A meander will be in a different position from where it was a century ago. Sediment is constantly being washed away from the bank on the outside of the curve. More sediment is being deposited on the inside, so the position of the meander is constantly changing. Sometimes the river cuts through the neck of the loop to form an ox-bow lake.

Most rivers display these three stages between their sources in the highlands and their mouths at the coast. However, all of them do not. A river in coastal mountains may be youthful all the way to the sea. A river may go through the stages at different times of its life. In a new mountain range, a river may be youthful throughout its length. As it gets older, it may be youthful at its source and mature at its mouth. Then, finally, as the land is worn down, the river will develop all three stages.

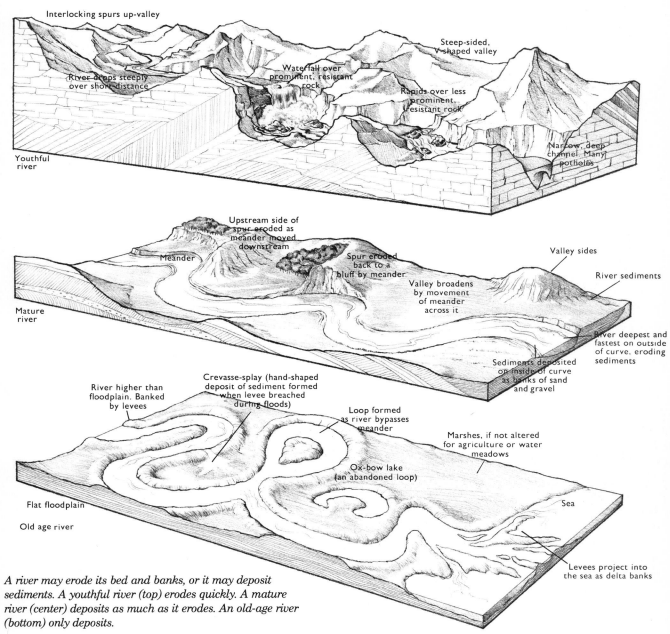

A river may erode its bed and banks, or it may deposit sediments. A youthful river (top) erodes quickly. A mature river (center) deposits as much as it erodes. An old-age river (bottom) only deposits.

GLACIERS

THE ICING THAT CHANGES THE CAKE

Scoop up a handful of snow and push it together into a snowball. The fluffy snow sticks together because the pressure of your hands turns the snow crystals into hard ice. This happens in nature, too.

In the mountains, snow falls every winter. The temperature does not rise enough to melt it in the summer. So, year after year, layer upon layer of snow builds up in the sheltered hollows. Eventually the snow becomes so thick that its weight squeezes down on the lower layers and compresses them into ice. This is the beginning of a glacier.

While ice is under pressure like this it can flow. It is difficult to imagine something as hard and brittle as ice actually twisting and flowing, but under great pressures even hard solids like rocks can be squeezed like toothpaste. This flowing ice can then move downhill, away from the sheltered hollow where it formed. It will follow any valley that it finds and then becomes a valley glacier.

The ice moving down the valley grinds down the rocks of the valley sides and bottom. It eventually carves out a deep, U-shaped channel. It will move down this channel until it reaches lowlands where the temperatures are higher. There the ice eventually melts.

The movement of a glacier is very slow. It may move only an inch or so a year, but its great weight makes it very powerful. The glacier moves faster at its center than at its edge. We cannot actually see the flowing ice. It is at the bottom of the glacier where the pressures are greatest. The ice on the surface is hard and brittle. It becomes cracked and torn by the movement of the ice beneath. This gives

The Ice Age

During the last two million years, ice caps covered most of northern Europe and North America. The ice advanced and retreated several times, with gaps of thousands of years in between. During the retreats, the climate was warmer than it is today. The ice sheets may well come back at some time in the future.

Ice sheets are vast and can cover entire continents. Today's major ice sheet covers Antarctica.

Valley glaciers, such as the Skilak glacier in Alaska (right), are restricted to U-shaped mountain valleys.

rise to deep cracks called crevasses and spiky pinnacles of ice called séracs. These features are most common where the glacier turns a corner or flows over a hump.

At high latitudes, near the North and South poles, glaciers can cover entire land masses. These are called ice sheets. We find them in Antartica, Greenland, and Iceland. Here the ice flows outward toward the sea, scraping up rocky material and carrying it along.

The emergence of ancient meteorites

At the edge of the Antarctic ice sheet, geologists have found meteorites that fell onto the ice sheet thousands of years ago. The meteorites were buried by later snowfalls and became incorporated into the ice itself. Eventually they were carried to the edge and melted out.

LANDSLIDES

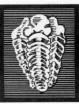

EROSION AT WORK

It is October 3, 1963. The calm waters of the Vaiont reservoir in northern Italy lie peacefully reflecting the slopes and forests of Mount Toc to the south. Suddenly the mountain moves. With a rumble that echoes around the surrounding peaks, 700 million cubic feet (20 million cubic meters) of the hillside crumble and fall into the lake. The impact of this hurtling mass of rock and soil sends up a wave, 656 feet (200 meters) high, that spreads outward from the scene of the collapse. The dam, 870 feet (267 meters) of towering concrete, stands unmoving. It resists the impact of the wave, but the water plunges over it and hurtles down the Longarone valley. Entire villages are swept away, and 2,600 people are killed.

How did this disaster happen? The water of the reservoir had seeped into the surrounding rocks. This lubricated the joints and bedding planes so that the slopes became unstable. The great masses of rock that formed the mountain could then slide over one another. This is the usual cause of the rapid erosional movements that we call landslides.

The most common type of landslide occurs where the layers of rock dip toward the open slope. When this happens the slope is very dangerous. If any supporting rock is moved from the bottom of the slope, the upper layers may come sliding down the bedding planes, lubricated by moisture that has seeped in.

Slumping is another familiar type of landslide. None of the original internal rock structures are involved in this. Where there is an exposed cliff of soft material, the rock or soil at the foot of the cliff is squeezed outward by the weight of the rock or soil above. This causes the cliff to collapse. The soil moves out, dragging the overlying masses down with it. The result is a series of curved slices. This produces a steplike structure of the ground at the top. The movement may be quite slow, taking several months. It may happen suddenly and disastrously.

A mudflow is a special kind of slump. It is produced in very loose material like mud or clay. An unstable slope may collapse in the usual curved slices like a normal slump, but it then forms a

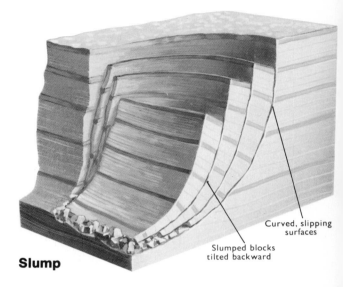

Slump

Curved, slipping surfaces

Slumped blocks tilted backward

jumbled tongue of disturbed other material that can flow. Everything in the path of such a flow is engulfed. This often happens in volcanic areas. The

Landslides are most often found on coasts. Waves constantly erode the bases of cliffs. The cliffs collapse as their support is lost. This example is in Dorset, southern England.

sides of an active volcano may consist solely of soft ash that has been spewed out of the vent by the eruption. A vast quantity of steam usually erupts from the volcanic vent. This falls as torrential rain.

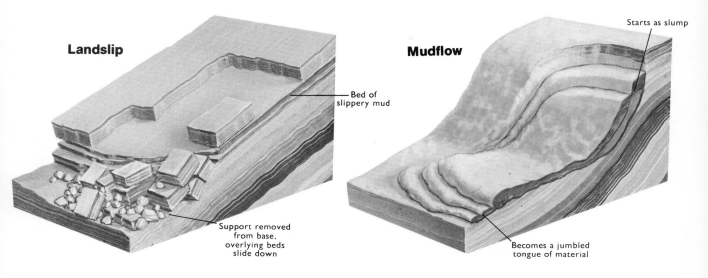

Landslip

Bed of
slippery mud

Support removed
from base,
overlying beds
slide down

Mudflow

Starts as slump

Becomes a jumbled
tongue of material

The powdery slopes soon become drenched and waterlogged. The resulting mud rushes downhill, adding to the volcanic disaster.

About a thousand years ago in Java, a 9,800–foot (3,000-meter) high volcano called Merapi slumped into a nearby valley. The valley was completely dammed. The jungles and temples of the valley, the home of a sophisticated civilization, were drowned in the lake that formed. In addition to this, the collapse of the volcano released the pressure that was holding down the hot magma beneath. Cataclysmic volcanic eruptions followed. To this day, the folk culture of Java has tales of the civilization that perished ten centuries ago.

Between 11 P.M. and midnight on November 13, 1985, the volcano of Nevado del Ruiz high in the Andes of Colombia erupted. It was one of the andesitic- type volcanoes and so the eruption was very violent. The heat that was generated melted the mountain snow and ice. The resulting water soaked the loose ash of the volcano's flanks, producing a liquid mixture. This poured down the mountain valleys at speeds of up to over 55 mph (90 km/h), swallowing up the town of Armero and killing over 20,000 people. Here survivors try to reach their trapped livestock across the engulfing mud.

CAVES

THE LAND BENEATH THE LANDSCAPE

The biggest cavern that we know about is in Sarawak, Malaysia. It is called the Lobang Nasip Bagus. It is 2,300 feet (700 meters) long, 980 feet (300 meters) wide, and is over 230 feet (70 meters) high. The aircraft carrier *USS Enterprise* could fit into this cavity crossways. There would still be room to maneuver the aircraft!

What could have made such a hole? As with most of the landscape features above the ground, the gentle rain is the culprit. However, the gentle rain is not as gentle as it may appear. While falling through the atmosphere, it dissolves the gas carbon dioxide and becomes an acid — carbonic acid. This acid reacts with certain minerals in the rocks of the earth's crust. The mineral calcite, which forms limestone, is particularly vulnerable and can be dissolved away quite easily. This accounts for the hollows, gorges, and caverns that are found in limestone areas.

Below a certain level beneath the surface of the ground, the rocks are completely saturated with water. The top of this saturated layer is called the water table. Much of the underground erosion of limestone areas takes place along and below the water table. Underground solution channels form. They produce tunnels in the shape of tributaries and meanders, just like those of rivers on the surface. Below this level, in the saturated zone, the acidic water dissolves away the limestone along cracks, joints, and bedding planes. If, for any reason, the water table lowers, then the tunnels formed by the underground solution system will be emptied of water and left as caves and galleries. Solution activity will continue at the new water table and below. Above the caves, the rock, broken up by solution cavities and cracks, is unstable. Roof collapses are frequent. Where underground water pours from one level to another, it dissolves out shafts called potholes.

Limestone caves often contain fantastic structures known as stalactites and stalagmites. These are also formed by acid water. This time, the water is redepositing the calcite that it has dissolved out

The hollows that are eroded out of limestone rock by the groundwater tend to be filled up again by deposition from the same groundwater. Stalactites and stalagmites grow imperceptibly by the constant deposition of minute grains of calcite. Over the millenia, these form fantastic structures such as those seen in the limestone regions of southeastern France (left).

Limestone caves

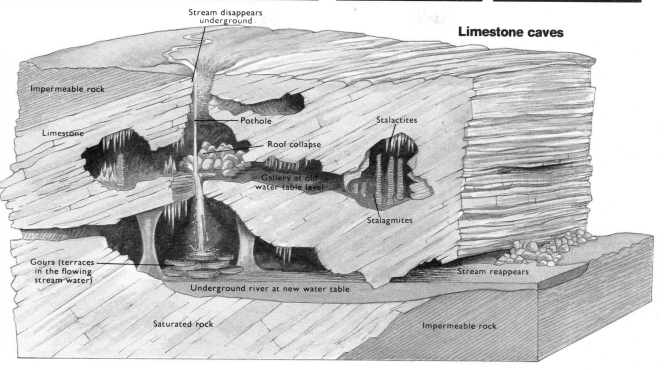

Stream disappears underground

Impermeable rock

Limestone

Pothole

Roof collapse

Stalactites

Gallery at old water table level

Stalagmites

Gours (terraces in the flowing stream water)

Stream reappears

Underground river at new water table

Saturated rock

Impermeable rock

of a rock. When a drop of groundwater hangs from the roof of a cave, the carbon dioxide tends to come out of it. This makes the water less acidic so it cannot hold so much calcite. The calcite is then deposited on the roof at that point. More calcite is deposited by later drops. An icicle shape called a stalactite is gradually formed. The biggest one that we know of is 195 feet (59 meters) long, in the Cueva de Nerja cave in Spain. The Statue of Liberty would not reach from its tip to its base!

A drop of groundwater falling to the floor of a cave will hit it with a splash. The shock of this will cause the calcite to fall out of solution. An upward growth, called a stalagmite, is formed there. There are all sorts of other structures formed by the redeposited calcite. Columns, curtains, and balconies form on the cave walls. Terraces form in the flowing water of the cave rivers.

A section through a cave system (above) shows a maze of horizontal tunnels and vertical shafts that mark the former courses of solution activity. Joints in the rock let the groundwater through and stalactites begin to form along these (right).

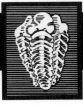

SOIL

THE FERTILE SCRAPINGS

The earth's crust is made of rocks. The rocks form the continents, the mountains, the plains, and all the other landscape features. However, it is not often that we see the rocks themselves. Usually they are covered with a loose material that enables plants to grow. This loose material is called soil.

Exposed rocks are constantly being broken down by rain and frost. Soil is basically the debris that results from all this destruction. Yet soil is more than rock fragments. It is full of dead plant material and chemicals produced by the decay of living things. It also contains living plants and animals, including bacteria and microscopic fungi, that are important for the formation of a fertile soil.

Let us look at a section of a typical soil. At the top, there is a layer of decomposing plant matter. This is known as the humus layer. Beneath this is the topsoil. Here humus is mixed with the mineral content of the soil. Groundwater seeps down from the surface and dissolves many of the minerals from this layer. The minerals are redeposited in the next layer down, the subsoil. Below the subsoil there is a fragmented rock layer. Here the underlying rock is being broken down. This layer lies directly on the parent rock.

The covering of soil can be very thick, or it can be thin or nonexistent. This depends mainly on the climate. Wet, tropical areas produce deep soils compared with cold, dry areas. This is because warm, moist conditions hasten the chemical reactions that break down the rocks. Such conditions also encourage the growth of vegetation that provides so much of the soil's substance.

A soil can be divided into a number of distinct layers called horizons (left).

Typical soil profile

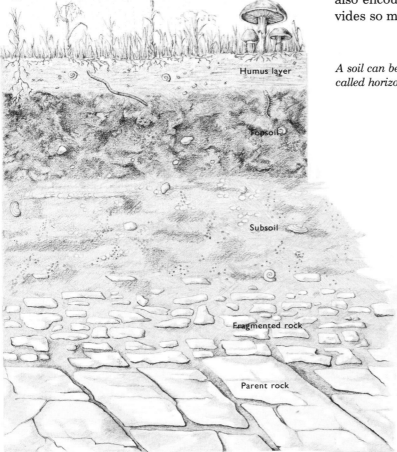

Humus layer

Topsoil

Subsoil

Fragmented rock

Parent rock

Peat (above) is a soil that is rich in plant material. Soils poor in plant matter are unstable and may blow away, as in the "dust bowl" of the 1930's (top).

Different rocks can produce different depths of soil. A hard, massive rock produces thinner soils than a soft, jointed, and easily eroded rock does. Soils on hillsides are thinner than soils on valley floors, because hillside soils are easily removed and washed away downslope.

Scientists recognize many different types of soil. The science of soil is called pedology and it is very complicated. Much of the pioneering work was done in the USSR. Because the composition of a soil affects the type and quality of crops that can grow in it, pedology is very important. Growing the wrong types of crops, or too much of them, can result in the soil losing its fertility and becoming barren. Sometimes an area of forest is cleared to make way for fields. Once the tree roots have gone, there is nothing to hold the soil together. It is easily washed away in the rain or blown away by the wind. The wrong kind of farming, resulting in the destruction of valuable topsoil, is one of the main causes of famine in the world today.

TROPICAL JUNGLE

HOT AND WET

Around the equator of the earth lies a band of tropical forest. Here it rains almost every day and the sun is constantly overhead. Conditions are hot and sticky and stiflingly humid. It is much like a greenhouse.

And, just as in a greenhouse, the plants can grow luxuriantly. Tall trees, up to 330 feet (100 meters) in height, reach up toward the sunlight, spreading their branches and leaves to the sky. They grow so closely that their boughs overlap, producing an almost continuous canopy of greenery far above the ground.

Beneath this canopy it is dark and gloomy. Because the topmost branches and leaves are so close together, very little light filters through. Bushes, shrubs, and undergrowth can grow only where light reaches the lower levels. This may happen along river banks or where a big tree has died and fallen, leaving a gap in the canopy. When such gaps appear, they do not last long. New trees germinate. Before long, a tree has grown to replace the lost giant tree. Again the forest floor is plunged into dim, misty twilight.

Animal life in the tropical forest is very varied. Much of it lives in the treetop canopy. Monkeys and apes swing in the branches. Butterflies flutter around the many glorious flowers. Birds of prey swoop and wheel between the boughs and trunks, dropping on unwary lizards and squirrels. Snakes lie in wait along the creepers, camouflaged among the greenery. On the thick forest floor, pigs and other compactly shaped animals live. They dart off between the massive trunks whenever danger threatens.

The constant heat and moisture helps the plants to grow so thickly. The temperature is 75–90°F (24–32°). The sun is almost always overhead and there are no seasons. The moisture is the result of the prevailing wind system, which brings 80 inches (200 centimeters) of rain. The rain is evenly distributed throughout the year.

Where the sun shines constantly, heating the ground, the air above the ground also heats up. This hot air, being lighter than cool air, rises. Cooler air then flows in to take its place. This gives rise to a

The prevailing trade winds (right) bring constant moist air to a region around the earth's equator. The heat and dampness produce dense tropical forests along this region except in the mountainous areas (map). The torrential rainfall feeds great rivers that wind through these jungle lowlands, such as in Brazil (above).

constant flow of wind toward the equator. These winds do not blow due north and due south, but are deflected to the west by the rotation of the earth. The resulting winds are the northeast trade winds and the southeast trade winds. Because these mostly blow over the ocean, they bring moisture to the equatorial regions. Then, when the air carried by them is heated and rises over the equator, the moisture carried condenses into clouds and falls as rain. The tropical rain forests result.

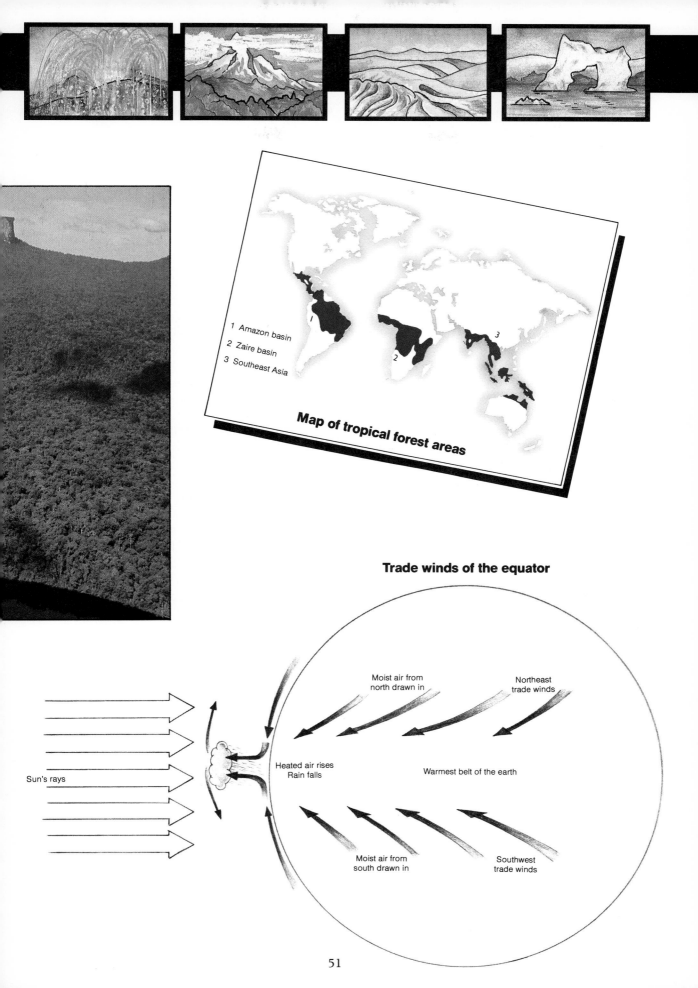

Map of tropical forest areas

1 Amazon basin
2 Zaire basin
3 Southeast Asia

Trade winds of the equator

Moist air from
north drawn in

Northeast
trade winds

Sun's rays

Heated air rises
Rain falls

Warmest belt of the earth

Moist air from
south drawn in

Southwest
trade winds

TROPICAL GRASSLAND

HOT AND VARIABLE

Wiry grasses yellow in the sun. The vast sweep of the plain shimmers in the midday heat. Here and there a thorn tree stands, black and flat on the top, like an umbrella. A black and white movement shows where a small herd of zebras is wandering toward a waterhole. Beyond them is the sandy color of a troop of gazelles. They are all oblivious of the lion, lazily watching them from the cover of the brittle grasses that form the main vegetation of this flat, open landscape.

A few hundred miles away, toward the equator, the luxuriant tropical forests grow. Why should there be such a difference in vegetation in such a short distance?

The earth's axis—the spindle around which it revolves—is not vertical to the sun. As the earth travels around the sun, the Northern Hemisphere is tilted toward the sun for half of the year. The Southern Hemisphere is tilted toward the sun for the other half. This is what causes the seasons.

When the sun is directly overhead, rain results. This is one reason tropical rain forests occur on the equator, where the sun is overhead for most of the year. On the tropical grasslands to the north and the south of the tropical rain forests, the sun is directly overhead for one season of the year only. This is the summer. Heavy rains fall during this season. For the rest of the year the winds are dry—just like those of the desert areas north of the northern grassland belt and south of the southern grassland belt. Grasses grow well in this kind of climate. They obtain all the moisture that they need in the one wet season. Very few trees grow in this climate because they need moisture for most of the year. These grasslands may have devastating fires during the dry season. This poses no problems for grasses because they can easily grow again from underground stems protected from the fires. Bushes and trees would be destroyed.

These broad grasslands support their own kinds of animals. Plant-eating animals must have strong teeth to eat grass, because the grass is tough. A grassland animal can see danger coming from a long way away. It needs long legs to run away from it. Thus, on grasslands, we see long-legged grazing animals such as zebras and gazelles. The kangaroos live in the same way on the grasslands of Australia. Their hunters must be swift movers as well. The hunters of the African plains are the lions and cheetahs.

In the summer, the trade winds bring moist air and rain to the grassland belt. Thus the wet season is the summer. In winter no moist air reaches the grasslands, so they have a dry season. The northern grassland belt is dry when the southern is wet, and vice versa.

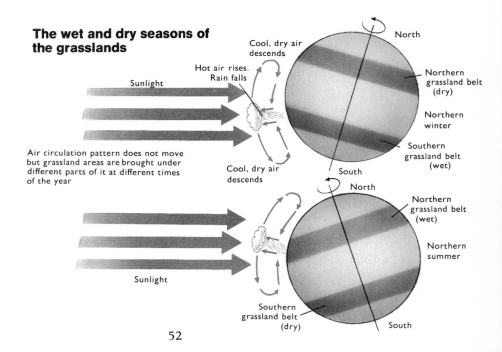

The wet and dry seasons of the grasslands

Sunlight

Hot air rises. Rain falls

Cool, dry air descends

Cool, dry air descends

Air circulation pattern does not move but grassland areas are brought under different parts of it at different times of the year

North

Northern grassland belt (dry)

Northern winter

Southern grassland belt (wet)

South

North

Northern grassland belt (wet)

Northern summer

Sunlight

Southern grassland belt (dry)

South

Map of grassland areas

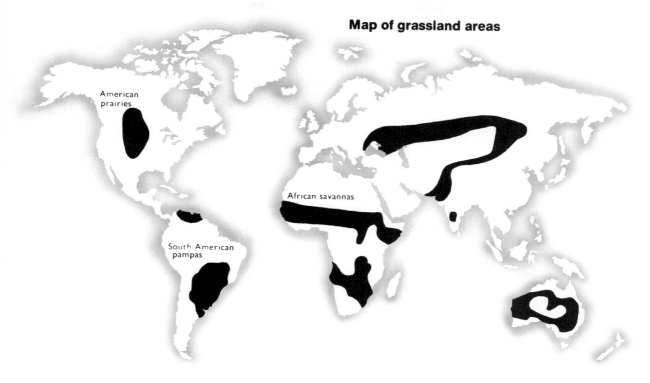

American prairies

African savannas

South American pampas

Long-legged animals, like giraffes, live on grasslands.
They can run from enemies that they can see from far away.

DESERTS

HOT AND DRY

Death Valley in California is thought to be the hottest place on the earth. Summer temperatures can reach as high as 134°F (56.7°C). The driest place in the world is probably central Australia, which may go for many years without rainfall. Both of these areas are desert areas.

The same wind systems that produce the tropical rain forests and the tropical grasslands are responsible for most of the deserts of our planet. The hot air that rises and drops its moisture over the equator spreads north and south at higher levels in the atmosphere. Eventually it cools and sinks back to the earth, roughly along the Tropics of Cancer and Capricorn. These descending air masses are dry, so they bring no rain to these areas. On reaching the ground, they spread toward the equator. There they become the trade winds once more. They also spread toward the poles, where they have an effect on the temperate climates of the world. As a result, two desert belts occur around the globe along the lines of the tropics. These desert belts contain the Mexican desert, the Sahara, and the Arabian desert in the Northern Hemisphere, and the Kalahari and Australian deserts in the Southern Hemisphere.

There are other types of deserts, too. Some places, in the middle of a continent, are so far from the sea that no moisture reaches them. The winds have dropped all their rain and have dried up before traveling that far. The Gobi Desert in the center of Asia is such a continental desert.

Sometimes the moist winds from the sea meet a coastal mountain range. The air is forced to rise as it passes over the peaks. Therefore all the rain falls on the side closest to the sea. This results in a rain shadow desert on the side of the range away from the sea. Death Valley was formed like this.

We usually think of deserts as vast, dry seas of sand. However, only about a fifth of the desert area of the world actually consists of rolling dunes

Map of desert areas

The deserts are in parallel bands on each side of the equator. They are constantly under the influence of descending dry air from the equator.

blows them around. This is the cause of most erosion in desert areas. A sandstorm, filled with millions of sand fragments, can blast exposed rock surfaces and wear them into all sorts of fantastic shapes. The rocky material that is worn away becomes more sand and takes part in further sandblasting.

Desert conditions are harsh. Very few animals and plants can survive there. The plants have adapted so they can survive without water for months or even years. Many are covered with tough, waterproof skin. Some are protected by spines to prevent animals from eating them. Others are covered with hairs to prevent water loss. Desert plants also have extensive root systems. Some may survive the drought by remaining dormant as seeds. Desert animals are also very highly adapted. Many live underground to protect themselves from the heat of the day and the chill of the night. They usually get all the water they need from the food they eat. They can use this water more efficiently than animals in other parts of the world. Camels can survive long periods without food and water. Fat stored in the hump is broken down to give them energy and water.

with rippled flanks and wisps of airborne sand streaming from the crests. Most desert areas consist of bare rock or flat expanses of pebbles and broken stone.

Sand forms because there is no moisture or decaying vegetable matter in the soil to hold it together. There are no plants to protect it from the wind. The wind lifts the dry soil particles and

The hot desert areas are found in two broken bands along the tropics (map). Along these lines, dry air descends from the upper atmosphere. The dryness means that little can grow here. The soil, lacking in vegetable matter, is sometimes no more than sand (right). When the sand is blown around, it erodes exposed rocks into fantastic shapes, as in Monument Valley in Utah (left).

Sand dunes

When masses of sand accumulate in the open air, they usually form sand dunes. These are curved heaps of sand that move under the influence of the wind. The wind blows sand grains up the gentle windward slope and deposits them down the steep lee slope. In this way, the dune travels across the sand, turning itself over as it goes. Lower crested dunes move more quickly. Because every dune is higher in the middle, each dune tends to form an arc shape, with the low points racing ahead of the high middle.

TEMPERATE CLIMATES
COOL AND VARIABLE

Winter comes as a sparkle of frost and a covering of snow. Plants do not grow and animals hibernate. In spring, the growing season begins. Seeds that have lain dormant in the ground over winter begin to put up shoots. Buds and leaves appear on the trees as the days become longer. In the summer, the days are long and warm. Trees are clothed in green, and vegetation everywhere is lush. The cooler days of autumn produce the golden reds of the leaves before they drop. Fruits and seeds appear. Then it is back to winter again, and nature closes down once more.

This is the annual sequence of events in the temperate latitudes. These are the regions of the earth's surface where it is neither blisteringly hot nor bitterly cold. Most of North America and Europe, parts of Asia, and the southern regions of South America and Australia can be classified as temperate.

A feature of temperate regions is the day-to-day variation of the weather. One day it may be cold and rainy. Another day it may be warm and sunny. The next day, a chill wind may be blowing. The reason for this is that the temperate regions lie at the junction of two great wind systems. In the Northern Hemisphere, where most of the temperate regions lie, cold air sweeps south-westward from the Arctic. Warmer air also blows northeastward from the tropics. These two air movements meet along a turbulent boundary. Where they curl and spiral around one another, forming what are known as frontal systems. Such frontal systems also occur in the Southern Hemisphere. There tropical air masses blowing southeastward meet cold air moving northwestward out of Antarctica.

The shearing movement of the two air masses sliding past each other in a frontal system sets up a series of eddies. These eddies are just like the little whirlpools you see in a river. The colder polar air is heavier than the warm tropical air. So the tropical air tends to rise above it. Moisture carried upward in this way condenses as clouds and falls as rain.

To complicate this pattern still further, many of the temperate areas lie by the sea. A great body of water, like the ocean, tends to hold its heat much longer than the land. The sea heats up slowly in the spring but it also cools slowly in the autumn. For this reason, coastal areas have much milder climates than areas just a few miles inland. Such areas are not as hot in summer or as cold in winter as the inland areas.

Frontal system

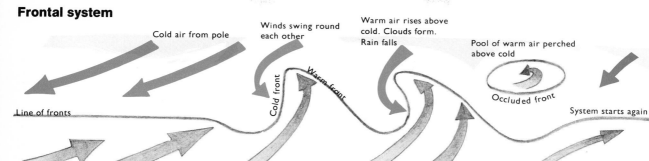

Cold air from pole

Winds swing round
each other

Warm air rises above
cold. Clouds form.
Rain falls

Pool of warm air perched
above cold

Cold front

Warm front

Occluded front

Line of fronts

System starts again

Warm air from tropics

Map of temperate areas

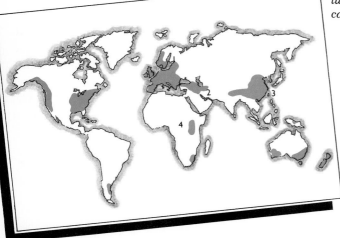

*Cold air from the poles meets warm
air from the tropics (map) in
turbulent frontal systems (above) and
causes variable weather.*

1   Temperate climate in
    cool latitude because
    of warm sea

2   Temperate climate at
    edge of extreme climate

3   Temperate climate in
    hot latitude because
    of cold sea

4   Equatorial temperate
    climate in mountains

Temperate region trees

Temperate regions are so called because the conditions are neither too hot nor too cold for a comfortable life. All kinds of plants and animals exist here, coping very well with the variable conditions. The redwood trees of western North America are the largest living things in the world. Some grow to heights of 300 feet (90 meters). The scientific name for these giant redwoods is *Sequoia.* The name comes from the great Cherokee chief Sequoya.

The world's tallest tree is in northern California. This redwood is 368 feet (112 meters) tall. It has a circumference of 44 feet (13 meters). The most massive living thing in the world is a giant sequoia called General Sherman. This too is in California. It has a circumference of 80 feet (24 meters) and is 267 feet (81 meters) tall. These are also very old trees. Redwoods can live for hundreds of years, but some of the giant sequoias are thought to be thousands of years old. One of the reasons for this is that these trees have thick bark up to 2 feet (0.5 meters) thick to protect them from insects and fungi.

*The trees of temperate lands can be
deciduous (far left) or coniferous
(above) such as these giant
redwoods.*

CONIFEROUS FORESTS

COLD AND DRY

The remote pine woods are great silent expanses of thick coniferous forest. Galleries of vertical, sticky trunks stretch into the blackness beneath the spreading boughs. There is no undergrowth. A thick of layer of decaying needles underfoot deadens any noise. Everywhere there is the smell of pine and resin.

These forests stretch in a broad band across the continents of North America, Europe, and northern Asia, just south of the Arctic Circle. The winters here are very cold and long. Any water is frozen as ice for most of the year and cannot be used by animals or plants. Anything living here must be able to cope with these harsh conditions.

Coniferous trees are well adapted to survive cold winters. They can flourish in a growing season lasting only three or four months. Their conical shapes can easily shake off the great weight of winter snow that would crush and break a tree of any other shape. Their leaves are in the form of needles—long and thin. Hardly any water evaporates from the needles because of their small surface area. The needles are coated with a thick, waxy sking that prevents the precious water from seeping out. A coniferous forest tends to have very few species of trees. Few species can survive the harsh conditions.

Few animals live in coniferous forests. Those that do are uniquely adapted to the conditions and climate. Only birds such as grouse can eat pine needles. Elk and deer eat the young shoots of the conifers. Beavers eat the bark. Small mammals, such as voles and lemmings, eat seeds from the cones and burrow away beneath the snow during the winter. The hunting animals of these regions are the wolves that hunt the deer, the lynxes that hunt that hunt the birds, and animals like weasels that hunt the small mammals.

It is the cold rather than a wind system that produces the conditions in which coniferous forests flourish. Coniferous forests are therefore also found in other parts of the world where there are the same temperatures. This is usually in mountain ranges. The higher up a mountain one travels, the cooler the conditions become. Most of the

Map of coniferous forests

The great belts of coniferous forest lie along the chilly northern reaches of the continents of North America, Europe, and Asia (map). The conical shapes of the coniferous trees are ideal for these climates. The trees can easily shake off the winter's snow and are not crushed by its weight (above). In the summer, large animals like moose browse in the vegetation of these cold regions (left).

mountain ranges of the world, including the Rockies, the Andes, the Alps, and the Himalayas, have coniferous forest zones. These forests are called montane forests to distinguish them from the boreal forests of the northern latitudes.

The great boreal forest of Europe and Asia is called the taiga. It stretches from western Norway to the Kamchatka peninsula on the eastern coast of Asia. It is 5,600 miles (9,000 kilometers) of uninterrupted coniferous trees.

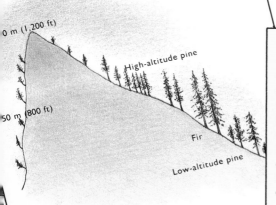

0 m (1,200 ft)

High-altitude pine

50 m (800 ft)

Fir

Low-altitude pine

Montane forests

There is a change of vegetation as you go away from the equator. The vegetation changes from tropical forest, through deciduous forest and coniferous forest, to ice cap. This is a zonation by latitude. There is also a similar zonation by altitude, with the same sequence found as you ascend mountains. Hence most mountain ranges of the world have a zone of coniferous forest at a particular height. Even within such a montane forest, the different species of conifer trees indicate small-scale variations of climate. The conifers that prefer a warmer climate grow farther down. Those adapted to chill conditions grow farther up.

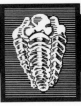

THE POLES

THE CHILL WASTELANDS

At the extreme north and south of our globe, the winters consist of six months of night. Temperatures can fall as low as $-126°F$ ($-88°C$). The summers consist of six months of sunlight, but the temperatures are still low.

At the North Pole there is the Arctic ocean. This is frozen and covered with ice that can be 160 feet (50 meters) or more thick. At the South Pole is the continent of Antarctica. This is also covered with ice and is almost totally barren. The few stretches of bare rock that peep through the frozen covering support only the hardiest of lichens and microorganisms.

The earth's axis is tilted at an angle or $23.5°$. The earth turns on this axis once a day. During the northern winter, the North Pole is tilted away from the sun. The earth's surface here does not see the sun at all during the winter. In the summer the North Pole is tilted toward the sun, so it is in daylight all the time.

The creatures that live in these extreme conditions depend largely on the sea for their food. Despite the freezing temperatures, the sea can support the growth of algae and the fish that feed on it. Seals and, in Antarctica, penguins feed on the fish. In the Arctic, polar bears hunt the seals.

In the Northern Hemisphere, a large area of land surrounds the Arctic ocean. Here conditions are a little less harsh—but not much. The surface of the ground thaws out on the surface during the summer. A few yards below the surface, the ground remains frozen and never thaws.

In a long winter the ground is covered by snow and ice. When summer comes, this melts, but it cannot drain away through the frozen soil below.

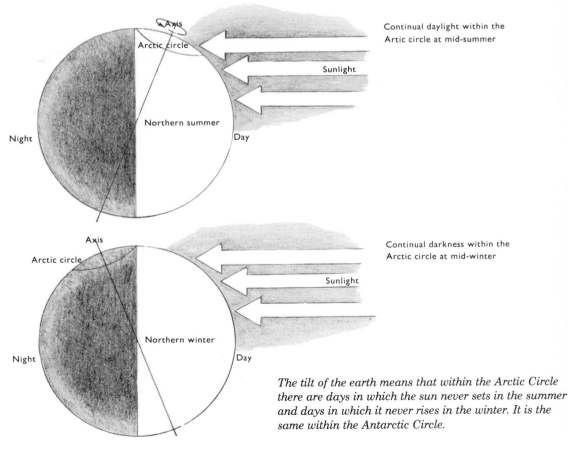

The tilt of the earth means that within the Arctic Circle there are days in which the sun never sets in the summer and days in which it never rises in the winter. It is the same within the Antarctic Circle.

Even in the barren ice-bound seas and islands around the North Pole there are creatures that thrive. Microscopic plants called plankton live in the sunny, upper layers of the water. This plant life feeds tiny animals such as shrimps. Shoals of these represent the food supply of Arctic fish. Fish are then caught by seals, which are, in turn, hunted by polar bears (left).

On the edge of the permanently frozen region lies an area that thaws out for a time in the summer. Plant life here consists only of lowgrowing shrubs and mosses and a few stunted trees. This region is called the tundra (right).

This frozen soil is called permafrost. Dreary marshes and shallow lakes form across the landscape. The vegetation that grows here consists mostly of hardy grasses, lichens, and mosses, and a few stunted birch trees. This landscape is known as the tundra.

Surprisingly, quite a number of animals live on the tundra. Insects swarm to take advantage of the short bright summer. The pools and lakes are filled with larvae. Adult flies and mosquitoes buzz around in dense clouds. Birds such as larks and martins migrate to these areas to feed on this insect bonanza. Ducks and geese flock here for the growth of water plants. In turn, these birds attract the attentions of predators, such as falcons and snowy owls.

Perhaps the most familiar mammal of the tundra is the reindeer. It wanders across the summer tundra plains, feeding on the lichen and mosses. In the winter it migrates to the dark coniferous forests farther south. This migration pattern is the basis for the way of the life of the Lapps. The Lapps are a nomadic Scandinavian people who follow the reindeer herds throughout their migrations. Apart from the reindeer, there was little in the tundra and Arctic regions to attract human settler. This changed when oil was discovered in Alaska.

COAL, OIL AND GAS

ANCIENT ENERGY

The energy that we use in our homes and our industry today was actually collected many millions of years ago.

Plants trap energy from the sun in their green leaves. They use this energy to make food from the carbon dioxide gas in the air and the water and minerals in the ground. The carbon dioxide is made up of carbon and oxygen. It is the carbon in this gas that is used. The oxygen is released back into the atmosphere. The food that is made is absorbed into the tissues of the plant. When the plant dies it decomposes back into carbon, water, and mineral substances. Oxygen from the air combines with the carbon to form carbon dioxide once more.

Alternatively, the plant may be eaten by animals and converted into animal matter. This then breaks down when the animal dies.

However, sometimes the dead plant and animal matter is buried so quickly that oxygen has no time to break it down. Deposits rich in carbon result. Vegetation buried by mud in a swamp will be compressed to form peat and, eventually, coal. Remains of microscopic animals buried at the bottom of the sea become deposits of oil. Both of these are very rich fuel supplies. Sometimes the coal and oil are broken down deep below the earth's surface and form natural gas. This gas is also a valuable fuel. Most of today's coal was formed during the Carboniferous Period from the lush forests that grew in humid swamps 300 million years ago.

These fuels are brought to the surface by mining or by drilling. They are then burnt to give energy. This burning breaks the substances down, combining the carbon with the oxygen of the air to form carbon dioxide, water, and minerals. This process would have happened in nature many millions of years ago if the material had not been buried quickly.

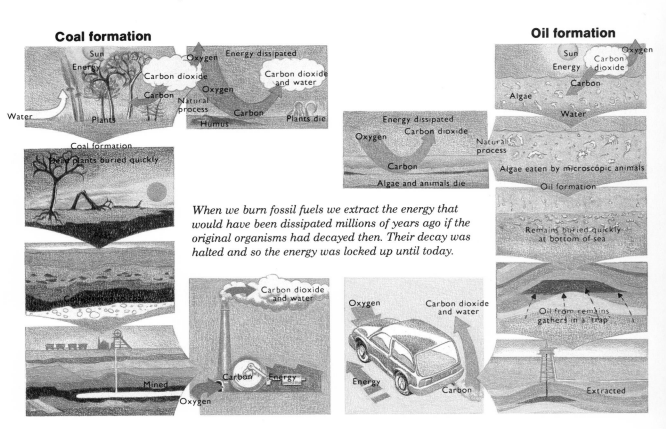

When we burn fossil fuels we extract the energy that would have been dissipated millions of years ago if the original organisms had decayed then. Their decay was halted and so the energy was locked up until today.

FOR FURTHER INFORMATION

You will find the following books useful if you want to learn more about any of the phenomena described on the previous pages.

ARDLEY, NEIL. *My Favourite Encyclopedia.* London: Hamlyn, 1984.

BARNETT, LINCOLN. *The World We Live In.* New York: Western Publishing, 1972.

BRAMWELL, MARTYN (Editor). *The Mitchell Beazley Atlas of the Oceans.* London: Mitchell Beazley, 1977

BRANLEY, FRANKLIN M. *Shakes, Quakes, and Shifts — Earth Tectonics.* New York: Thomas Y. Crowell, 1974.

BROCARDO, G. *Minerals and Gemstones.* Newton Abbot: David and Charles, 1982.

CLARK, A. *Minerals* (Hamlyn Nature Guides). London: Hamlyn, 1979.

DINELEY, DAVID. *Earth's Voyage Through Time* London: Granada, 1975.

DINELEY, DAVID, HAWKES, DONALD, HANCOCK, PAUL & WILLIAMS, BRIAN. *Earth Resources* (Arrow Reference Series). London: Arrow, 1976.

DIXON, DOUGAL. *Geography* (Franklin Watts Science World Series). London: Franklin Watts, 1983.

DIXON, DOUGAL. *Geology* (Franklin Watts Science World Series). London: Franklin Watts, 1982.

DIXON, DOUGAL. *Minerals, Rocks & Fossils* (The Nature Detective Series). London: Macdonald, 1984.

DUNNING, F. W., MECER, I. F., OWEN, M. P., ROBERTS, R. H. & LAMBERT, J. L. M. *Britain Before Man.* London: Her Majesty's Stationery Office, 1978.

Focus on Earth Science. Columbus, Ohio: Merrill Publishing, 1984.

GASS, I. G., SMITH, PETER J., & WILSON, R. C. L. *Understanding the Earth.* London: Open University/Artemis, 1972.

HOLMES, ARTHUR. *Principles of Physical Geology.* London: Nelson, 1978.

JANULEWICZ, MICHAEL A. *The International Book of the Forest.* London: Mitchell Beazley, 1981.

LAWRENCE, J. T. *Fossils.* Worthington, Ohio: Willowisp Press, 1987.

MATTHEWS, WILLIAM. *Introducing the Earth: Geology, Environment, and Man.* New York: Dodd, Mead, and Company, 1972.

MERCER, CHARLES. *Monsters in the Earth: The Story of Earthquakes.* New York: G. P. Putnam's Sons, 1978.

MUIR WOOD, ROBERT. *On the Rocks.* London: BBC, 1978.

The Planet Earth. Chicago: World Book, 1984.

REDFERN, R. *Corridors of Time Orbis.* London: 1980.

RETCHIE, DAVID. *The Ring of Fire: Volcanoes, Earthquakes, and the Violent Shore.* New York: Atheneum, 1981.

ROBSON, D. A. *The Science of Geology.* Poole: Blandford, 1968.

SMITH, DAVID G. *The Cambridge Encyclopaedia of Earth Sciences.* Cambridge: Cambridge University Press, 1981.

THACKRAY, JOHN. *The Age of the Earth.* London: Her Majesty's Stationery Office, 1980.

VAN ROSE, SUSANNA. *Earthquakes.* London: Her Majesty's Stationery Office, 1983.

Picture Acknowledgements

Barnaby's Picture Library 56, 57; BBC Hulton Picture Library 25 bottom, 49 Bettman Archive; British Museum (Natural History) Geological Museum 30; Bruce Coleman Ltd: 10 N. Devore, 14/15 B.J. Coates, 23 A.P. Davies, 29 J. Burton, 35 Sullivan & Rodgers, 39 K. Gunnar, 40 top G. Cubitt, 42/43 F. Erize, 50/51 M. Freeman, 54 M. Fogden, 61 bottom M.P. Harris; Dougal Dixon 27 top left; Eric Hosking 61 top; Geoscience Features Picture Library 11, 13 bottom, 22/23, 31, 38 left, 38/39, 46, 48/49, 59 top; HGPL endpapers, 25 top; Eric Kay 13, 44; Frank Lane Picture Agency: 17 S. McCutcheon Alaska Pict. Service, 18, 19 USDA Forest Service, 27 bottom M. Newman, 43 S. McCutcheon, 58 H. Rhode; Rex Features 45 El Tiempo; RIDA Picture Library/D. Bayliss 9, 27 top right, 47; Seaphot/Planet Earth Pictures 20 H. Jones, 55 J. Lythgoe; Jeremy Tyler/Department of Earth Sciences Cambridge University 36.

Reproduced by permission of the Director, British Geological Survey (NERC): Crown/NERC copyright reserved 24, 28, 37, 40.

Front cover
Bruce Coleman Ltd: Kilanea-Iki Volcano, Hawaii; inset top Monument Valley, USA; inset bottom Apophyllite crystals.
Back cover
Seaphot/Planet Earth Pictures: Iceberg, Greenland.
Title Page
Geoscience Features Picture Library: the Alps in winter.
Half-title page
HGPL: Giant's Causeway, N. Ireland.
Artists
Sally-Anne Grover; Kevin Maddison; Oxford Illustrators Ltd; Tony Payne.

INDEX

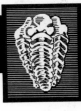

Figures in *italic* type refer to illustrations.